Generis
PUBLISHING

Anthology of Economic Studies

Teimuraz Beridze

Title: **Anthology of Economic Studies**

ISBN: 979-8-89248-406-0

Author: Teimuraz Beridze

Cover image: pixabay.com

Publisher: Generis Publishing
Online orders: www.generis-publishing.com
Contact email: info@generis-publishing.com

Contents

To wife Tamara, daughters Eliso and Sophia

Foreword

The present collection is an anthology of articles published by the author in recent years; its architectonics presents not chronological, but the actuality problems, in particular - the transitional period in economy and economic reforms in the post-Soviet society (The Case of Georgia); property relations and management; the role of the subjective factor in the economy; the economic and legal aspects of property; qualitative and quantitative aspects of economic growth; international studies of the workforce; the investment potential of the economy; crime and punishment: an economic approach; and others.

I think a collection of mentioned articles will be interesting and important for people interested in economic issues.

Teimuraz Beridze

June, 2024

The Republic of Georgia: Problems of Transition to a Market Economy

Background in the Country

The Land

The former Soviet Republic of Georgia is a country spanning some 26,911 square miles in the Trans-Caucasus region to the south of the towering Caucasus Mountain range. In 1989 the population of Georgia, which then included the regions of Abkhazeti and South Ossetia, stood at 5,443,359. The ethnic composition of the republic situated between Russian to the north, Turkey and Armenia to the south, and Azerbaijan to the southeast is a mosaic depicting its rich and turbulent history. The Black Sea provides Georgia's economic and cultural gateway to the West. Significantly, the Abkhazeti region occupies half of this spectacular and fertile coastline.

In western Georgia, the lowlands are home to tea and citrus production, while the highlands are abundant with grapes and deciduous fruit. Eastern Georgia, with a drier climate, has lowlands fit for grape production. The wines of Georgia, which come in many varieties, are highly valued on the international market, and are often awarded top prizes at exhibitions. The climate of Georgia produces warm summers and relatively mild winters. The environmental attractions of Georgia are plenty, with many natural game preserves, caves, waterfalls, lakes, mountain streams, beautiful valleys, and snow-capped mountain peaks. Georgia also has several mineral springs, world-renowned for their therapeutic capabilities. The most popular ones are in Borjomi, Sairme, and Zvare. Minerals such as manganese and coal abound in the mountainous reaches, in addition to precious metals.

History

The Georgian people were besieged by their neighbors over the course of eleven centuries, from the seventh to the eighteenth. The late eleventh century is when Georgia was hit with invasion from a destructive band of Central Asians called the Seljuk Turks. The reigning king of Georgia, King Giorgi II, abdicated the throne in favor of his 16-year-old son, who became King David IV, called "the Builder." With small, mobile army units, the Kartveli' regained their territory slowly and worked to return the land to its former fertility. The king then improved his army to sufficient strength and, in 1124, united most of the Trans-Caucasus region. The great king died the next year, but his successors expanded the kingdom even further. This time, between the Seljuk Turks' defeat through the thirteenth century saw the golden age of Georgia. However, the Mongol invasion in the late thirteenth century was their downfall. King Giorgi V threw off the Mongol yoke after several decades and reunited forces of Tamerlane ("Timur the lame") invaded Georgia eight times with the same ruthlessness as the Mongols, but they did not assume political power over the Georgians. In 1453, the Ottoman Turks seized the Byzantine city of Constantinople, the trade link between Christian lands of Georgia and Italy. Georgia found itself surrounded by hostile Muslim neighbors, as Ottoman influence flowed into the northern Caucasus. After eleven centuries of mixed fortunes, the Kartveli, looking for peace, turned to religious northern neighbor Russia. Russia quickly annexed Georgia and exiled the royalty in 1801. This setback did not prevent the development of Georgian culture, despite the removal of the Georgian language by Russian decree. Georgia never gave up the fight for independence, and regained its sovereignty in 1918, only to be reclaimed by the communist Union of Soviet Socialist Republic (USSR) in 1921. After 70 years of Soviet rule, Georgia proclaimed itself a republic in April 1991.

The Populace

Georgia is currently the home of approximately 5.5 million people of many different nationalities. The ethnic composition of Georgia is: 68.8% Georgian (including several regional subgroups speaking distinct languages in addition to Georgian, for example Mengrelians, Svanetians - ethnic groups), 9% Armenian; 7.4% Russian: 5.1% Azerbaijani; 3.2% Ossetian; 1.9% Greek, and 1.7% Abkhazetian. Most of the population is of the Christian faith (followers of the Georgian Orthodox church) but Islam is professed by the people of Ajaria in southwest Georgia, by Azerbaijanis in southeastern Georgia, and by the small population of Kurds.

About 56% of the population lives in the urban areas, and one-third of them reside in the capital city, Tbilisi. Tbilisi is the industrial and cultural center of the nation. It is also one of the oldest cities in the world, being more than 1,500 years old. Tbilisi is on the same latitude as Istanbul, Rome, Barcelona, and Chicago, and has an average annual temperature of 13.2°C.

The Culture

In the 4th century AD, Georgia adopted Christianity. Since then, the state religion has been Orthodoxy. From this, Georgians receive their mentality and spiritual values. At the same time, Georgians have also been tolerant of other religions practiced within the country.

The Georgian language is one of the oldest languages in the world, over 2,000 years old. It is a member of the Iberio-Caucasian group of languages, and has its own alphabet -one of only fourteen alphabets in the world. The ancient city of Phasis, currently called Poti, was the home of a school of rhetoric attended by both Georgians and non-Georgians, and is highly praised in Greek history. Despite Georgia's small size, it is home to more than 20,000 cultural monuments, many of which are based on religion or mythology. There are also many historical monuments. Popular Georgian authors include Shota Rustaveli, Ilia Chavchavadze.

The Economy

Georgia is a resource rich country. There are approximately 300 known mineral ores in the Republic; a bit more than half of which are currently being utilized. The principal mineral resource is manganese. There are also substantial reserves of carbonates and clay for production of cement and other construction materials. Total coal reserves are 400 million tons and known oil reserves are 27.5 million tons. About 40% of the land area is agricultural, and 40% is forested.

Georgia was among the first republics of the Former Soviet Union (FSU) to declare independence, doing so April 9,1991. Although official pre-independence statistics on per capita income ranked Georgia relatively low among the republics of the FSU, it was in fact relatively well-off due in part to a strong tradition of entrepreneurship and an agricultural sector with significant private sector activity. The Republic had the highest proportion of college graduates among the republics of the FSU and one of the highest levels of saving deposits.

In 1989-1991, industry accounted for 37% of Net Material Product (NMP) and agriculture for 33% somewhat more than in the other FSU republics. The main products included agriculture (citrus, tea, wines), Agri-Industry (processed foods, fertilizers), and natural resources, notably manganese. Georgia was also a relatively large producer of steel-pipes, electric motors, synthetic fibers, roofing materials, textiles, and shoes. The tourist subsector was well developed due to Georgia's geographical location, attractive climate, and abundance of agricultural products. Exports included wine, tea, citrus, mineral water, manganese, and light industrial products, Georgia was heavily dependent on imports of both raw materials and energy from other republics.

The Georgian economy was an integral part of the centrally planned economy of the Soviet Union. Plan was constructed and production quotas were established on the basis of Union-wide requirements, and raw materials and other inputs were sourced throughout the Union. Financial and barter clearance were organized on a Union-wide basis. Georgia's industrial structure reflects these Union arrangements. It was the designated producer of wine, tea, and citrus, but not of grain and other agricultural products. It has a number of industrial organizations (including steel and locomotives) equipped for Union-wide supply. Georgian energy resources are under- developed as a result of preference given to resources elsewhere in the Union. A major part of the process of economic reform lies in adaptation of this structure to the requirements of international competition.

Since independence in 1991, the Georgian economy has been in a severe decline. A break down in traditional trade and payments relations with other FSU countries, civil conflict and the war in Abkhazeti, and expansionary financial policies have combined to cause a collapse in output, massive inflation and currency substitution, and a large external debt. The population's living standards have declined sharply, and the country has had to rely on external aid to help meet its most basic needs.

While they may underestimate private market activity, official estimates show NMP declining 21% in 1991, 43% in 1992, and 40% in 1993. Since 1989, industrial production has declined approximately 75%, agricultural production has declined about 55% and construction activity has virtually ceased. Real exports and imports have fallen sharply. Unfortunately, these tendencies have been continued in 1994 and partly in 1995.

Contributing factors in the economic decline include a number of factors common to all small, energy-importing republics of the FSU; the disruption of trade with the other republics sharply higher energy prices and difficulties in obtaining key imports. The increase in energy prices was devastating as the price of imported oil and natural gas increase over 500% in dollar terms between 1990 and 1993. In addition, problems unique to Georgia have worsened the economic situation. The war in Abkhazeti forces dome 270,000 refugees to flee their homes placing a severe burden on the economy. The war directly affected Georgia's citrus and tea export crops and decimated the tourism industry. Civil strife and a deterioration of law and order in 1992 and 1993 disrupted the economy and consumed the Government's attention.

Fortunately, the political and social situation in the country has improved considerably over the last year although the economic situation has not. The war in Abkhazeti has ceased. While progress to date has been disappointingly slow, Georgia has consistently sought a peaceful resolution of the Abkhazeti conflict and the peaceful return of the refugees to their homes. Actions implemented in the spring of 1994 have resulted in a sharp reduction in the criminal activity. The improvement in the political and social situation has enabled the Government to turn its full attention to solving the economic crisis. With the assistance of the World Bank (WB), International Monetary Fund (IMF), and other international agencies and bilateral donors we are determined to do so, The impact of the economic decline on the Georgian population has been considerable. Even with a substantial rise in private sector employment, total employment has declined approximately 30% since 1990. In addition, hidden unemployment is widespread. Wages of most workers in the state sector, as well as pentanes and unemployment compensation, was less than a US$2-3 per month. While many are able to supplement this wage with private sector activity, many can not. Natural gas and electricity are rationed and central heating was discontinued in 1993. From January 12, 1995 the Government halted gas supply to the population (households) because only 9% of due payments were paid by them. Many rural families have been able to switch to wood heat but this is creating a problem with deforestation. Most rural residents are without electricity and urban residents are subject to extended blackouts.

While the situation has improved dramatically in recent months, the Georgian economy has also been beset with hyperinflation. Process increased approximately 60% a month from mid- 1993 through mid- 1994. The foreign exchange value of the Georgian coupon declined accordingly. Shortly after it was issued in April 1993, the Georgian coupon traded at 700 coupons per US$1. As a result there has been widespread currency substitution. The US Dollar and Russian Ruble (Russian Federation Currency) were used in most private market transactions. The Government of Georgia recognized that this inflation is primarily the result of the fiscal policies followed in recent years. In the past the Government had little alternative to large budget deficits due to the large economic and social problems faced by the Government and reduced ability to collect taxes due to the civil unrest and decline in the Government's authority. As outlined below, steps are now being taken to reduce our budget deficit. Later the inflation has lessened and the foreign exchange value of the coupon has stabilized.

Georgia joined the WB and IMF in 1992 and began reform programs in cooperation with both institutions shortly thereafter. Unfortunately, both these relationships and our reform program were interrupted by the war and accompanying breakdown of law and order. With the return of social stability, our relationships with the Bretton Wood institutions were re-established early 1994 and we have been working closely with them to stabilize and reform the Georgian economy. In December 1994, Georgia received the first tranche of Systematic Transformation Facility (STF) from the IMF. Now we have enhanced the STF arrangement to standby loans covering 1995-1996; and the WB supports macroeconomic stabilization and structural reform programs by providing Georgia with Rehabilitation credit and numerous other credits in the transport, agriculture, municipal, service, health care, education, energy development sectors.

Economic Reform: First steps and Results

Both theory and history shed little light on the process of transition from central planning and administrative control to a market-oriented economy. Economic theory, being chiefly concerned with equilibrium, hus little to say on how to proceed from one state, let alone from one system, to another. Even the relevant subject of comparative economic systems fail to enlighten us on this matter. Nor do we get much help from history. So far, no centrally planned economy of the FSU has managed to make the transition to a well-functioning market system.

The collapse of the state was a strong argument for what is called "shock therapy," but might be better labeled "big bang" reform in a FSU area. Jeffery Sachs of Harvard University justifies this approach by pointing to the three interrelated economic crises that confront post-communist countries: state bankruptcy, systematic collapse, and structural transformation. The first shows itself in default and inflation, the second in the disinterpretation of state economic control, and the third in the shrinkage of the over-emphasized heavy-industrial sector. "The aim of shock therapy," argues Prof. Sachs, "is to address these three crises via the rapid introduction of the core institutions of capitalism." These are private property, a stable, convertible currency, freedom for trade and international investment; corporate control of large enterprises; and, a social safety act

The "Shock Therapy" approach means three interrelated measures: 1) Liberalization; 2) Stabilization; and, 3) Structural Policies.

A country that truly followed the rapid-change approach would satisfy most of the following conditions:

- Prices were freed rapidly and pervasively;
- Tough restriction of income of the population;
- Considerable increase of interest rate and restriction of money supply in circulation;
- Increase of interest rate of cash and other deposits aimed to stimulate the population to save;
- Monetary stability and fiscal responsibility resulted in low inflation rates;
- Issuing bonds of government loan aimed to cover the state budget deficit;
- An efficient tax system replaced the inefficient and distortionary implicit taxation of command economy;
- Full currency convertibility, without restrictions and controls;
- Introducing common customs tariff in order to restrict import and stimulate export;
- A social safety net was created with reasonable rules and conditions that provided for subsistence living but discouraged taking advantage of the system;
- Active competition replaced monopolistic supply of goods and services.

"Shock Therapy" in GEORGIA

The use of "shock therapy" method began in Russia in January 2, 1992. A month later it began in Georgia:

- The price reform started in Georgia in Spring 1991 when free prices on some types of goods were introduced. In February 1992 there were radical changes in the price formation system in Georgia: the prices of one group of goods and services were entirely freed, and the regulated prices of another group increased considerably. All these measures were aimed to balance the market. In 1991 the consumer price index was 1.8; in 1992 it reached 25. Regulated consumer prices increased 68 times in 1992 in comparison with those of 1991;
- At the starting of reform (1992) there was no national currency in Georgia, only form April 1993 when Georgia introduced its own (intermediate) currency "coupon" the government got the change to

conduct its own monetary policy. The "coupon" was issued in April 93 at par with the ruble, trading at about 700 coupons per USD shortly after issue. In late 1994 the rate was over 2 million coupons per USD. In early 1995 the rate fell to 1.3 million USD. The Russian ruble exchange rate has moved from over 1,000 coupons per ruble in late 1994, to 300 coupons per ruble in 1995;

- The rate of inflation accelerated from around 5 percent in 1990 to 175 percent in 1991, 1,340 percent in 1992, 5,040 percent in 1993, and 8,380 percent in 1994, Stabilization measures have brought the rate down sharply month-to-month inflation in 1995 when real new Georgian national currency ("Lari") has introduced (1 Lari 1 million coupon; 1 USD 1,24-1.26 Lari; 1 Lari 4,000 Russian rubles) prices increased 25-30% but now they reached some equilibrium and inflation is on average 1% a month;
- From 1991 there began to be indexation of minimal wages and social donations in Georgia. In in 1991 the indexation was made only once, but in 1992 in the process of started liberalization of price formation the income indexation was made six times. In 1991 the minimum and average wage of employees increased in comparison with that of previous year by 1.85 times and 1.26 times, respectively. In 1992, as compared to 1991, the multiply by 13.14 times and 17.94 times correspondingly. True, no strict regulating measures were conducted in Georgia by means of which it might be possible to increase the wage fund (as it was made in Poland when in case of 2% overspending of wage fund the penalty was imposed on an enterprise equal to 200% of this sum; and if the overspending was more than 2% the penalty was 300- 500% of corresponding sun) but the increase of wages and social donations fell behind the price increase;
- Interest rate on deposits increased from 2% in 1991 to 5% in 1992, and for 10 years deposits the interest rate increased from 9% to 80%. Such increase of interest rate did not reflect the inflation rate. It should also be noted that it was impossible to restrict the money supply in. circulation in Georgia of those days by increasing the interest rate, because there was no monetary system of its own in Georgia; there was the ruble of the already disintegrated USSR, and new Russian ruble in calculation in Georgia. At the starting of reform (1992) there was no national currency in Georgia, only from April 1992 Georgia introduces her own (intermediate) currency "coupon";

- In summer of 1992 it was decided to double cash deposits on an anticipated payment basis. In particular, in July 25 the decision was made to double the devaluated cash deposits in accordance with the state for August 1. The decision was made to prolong the time for placing money on cash deposits for only after I year. As an exception this money should be used in the process of privatization.

- As it became rather difficult to receive in time adequate quantity of bank-notes from Russia in the second half of 1992 the money accumulated in this way was paid out on wages and pensions, and this practically excluded the restriction of money supply by the government;
- In 1992 the specific role of government investments in total expenditure of the state budget was not reduced. Till 1992, it fluctuated within the limits of 20-25%. The actual quantity of subsidies in 1992 in comparison with those of 1991 increased by about 5.1 times. True, in 1991 the specific weight of subsidies in budget expenditure constituted 47% and in 1992 it reduced to 30.1%;
- Government internal premium bonds were issued in 1992. But they were offered for sale only in autumn of 1993 and mainly in order to change bond of the former Soviet Union to new Georgian bonds. As to the use of government bonds to meet a lack in the state budget deficit, it should be noted that it hasn't started in Georgia yet;
- Tax system regulation adequate to market economy started in Spring 1991;
- In 1992 blanket customs tariffs were introduced; 2% was levied on import and 8% on export. It was evident that this situation did not favor the import restriction on import and export stimulation. That is why item nine of the "Balcerowicz Plan" was not realized in Georgia either;
- In 1992, there was no national currency in Georgia, and so it was impossible to realize "full currency convertibility" require;
- It was already mentioned above that in 1992 in the same way as in 1991 there was income indexation. At that time any type of assistance to families with low income was not taken into consideration. That is to say, the social protection system did not contain in itself mechanism. For example, all incomes are doubled, the absolute discrepancy in income between those having high and low income is increased, because the discrepancy itself was subjected to doubling. (If one person's wage is 100

rubles and another person's wage constitute 150 rubles and the second person's wage 300 rubles; the discrepancy between wages is also subjected to doubling: 50 rubles rises up to 100 rubles). Thus, in condition of total income indexation the situation of families with low income worsens. As a result of this the actual minimum wage in 1992 constituted only 86% of that of 1991;

- In 1992, for the first time in Georgia, legal and government resolutions restricting monopolistic institutions and developing competition were issued. Their full scale implementation in the same year naturally were not realized. In general in Georgia were not realized also such important measures of the a "Shock Therapy." as canceling of budgetary subsidies and tough restriction of money supply. It should also be mentioned that many of those items were doomed to failure, first of all, because there was no monetary system at that time in Georgia. In these conditions the carried out "Shock Therapy" method based only on price liberalization was condemned to failure. In other words, in absence of corresponding governmental institutions the transition to market economy with the help of "Shock Therapy" method was practically impossible. In this situation, it might be much more correct to choose the step-by-step way for the transition to market economy which could be based on consecutive creation of institutions necessary for reforms and statehood on the whole.

Reform Difficulties

One reasons for the difficulties of economic reform is political factor and another is the result of a wrong economic policy. Economy of Georgia (and not only economy) was not ready for carrying out full-scale military operations started in Abhazeti in summer of 1992 and for unleashing the civil war in autumn of 1993. It resulted in actual derangement of the state budget: in 1993-1994 there was no previously approved budget in Georgia.

The only possible source was money emission to cover the discrepancies between the state expenditures and revenues: in 1993 the state expenditures exceeded tax revenues 1.118 billion coupons and in 1994 it amounted to 28,293 billion coupons.

First artificially (by means of granted amnesty in winter of 1992) and then (second) by participation in military operations (as a country without army) aggravated the criminal situation in Georgia, and it made it dangerous to conduct any economic activity. As a result of it many businessmen left their native country, robbery was replaced by racketeering, which also does not create favorable conditions for business development. These criminals could not on the whole manage to accumulate fortune and namely many amassed by means of undisguised robbery and racketeering (it could, in future put the people, who became rich in this way, in a position, when they need stable situation in the country to realize to advantage of the accumulated property).

At the end of 1992 and at the beginning of 1993 the most noteworthy mistake, out of the errors was that the government, for some reason, did not expect that it would not receive banknotes of cash money from Moscow. That is why the government had to bring into circulation the temporary banknotes of Georgia - the coupon of the National Bank of the Republic of Georgia (NBG). It is noteworthy that representatives of different levels of authority revealed not serious, and in some cases, contemptuous attitudes towards coupon, resulting in decisive influence on intensification of devaluation process. Basically, the temporarily or constantly within the desired, for some people, "ruble zone." That is why the coupon was announced the only legal tender of payment not at the beginning buy only when Russian in July-August of 1993 carried out partial currency reform and withdrew from circulation the ruble of the disintegrated Soviet Union.

Uncontrolled credit emission laid down the foundation of inflationary process in Georgia, and the attempts to solve agricultural problems on the account of practically non-existent budget since autumn 1993 (procurement of agricultural products in autumn of 1993 and carry out of agricultural work in spring of 1994), resulted in unseen for that period budget emission and it finally deranged the financial system of the country and Georgia turned out to be in the hyperinflationary spiral: inflation rate in 1993 till autumn of 1994 constitute 60-70% per month. In the long run this money was not unfortunately used for agricultural purposes. In condition of high inflation rate the coupon did not perform the function of turnover servicing, because real value of the coupon supply was constantly reducing. Other things being equal, it promoted the range of use of the ruble (Russian monetary unit) instead of the coupon as means of payment.

The policy of the NBG towards restriction of cash money circulation area (which caused, devoid of common sense, restriction on the withdrawal of the cash coupon from the bank system) resulted in considerable discrepancies between cash and non-cash money values. It resulted in maximum restriction of the coupon circulation area. State commercial banks proceeding to work in overdraft conditions promoted hidden credit emission. Subsidized prices on bread, gas, electricity, transport gave budget an additional "loading" and it also promoted budget emission.

A blunder was made in foreign trade which manifested in consolidation of the "unique Georgian" clearing. Barter was considered the only way to receive gas from Turkmenistan. The prices on both Turkmenistan gas and a lot of poor quality goods produced in Georgia were artificially overcharged. According to "innovators" of such approach it should result in creation of environment for Georgian enterprises stimulating their activity. It should be mentioned that such environment for producing goods of poor quality has really been created. At the same time this production had to be purchased by government on budget expense. In the absence of budget this operation has been carried out only partially, and even then due to moncy emission (and it also promoted inflation). The biggest part of this production was withdrawn under compulsion by government from enterprises giving a guarantee to pay corresponding price in future. Thus, putting these enterprise in difficult financial situation a resulted in forming non-payment "network" within the country, which was difficult to ruin. For the government it was impossible to collect full volume of goods within the country, because commodity exchange by barter was envisaged by agreement with Turkmenistan. In recent years the existing difficulties on Azerbaijan transport artery, first by blocking railroad passing through Abkhazeti and then through Chechnya, first complicated, and then made impossible duty transportation of goods, collected by government, to Turkmenistan. As a result of all this during two years Georgian's debt to Turkmenistan amounted to about half a billion USD.

To start the mentioned mechanism of interstate turnover of goods the system of state order was used, which required the complicated system of quotation and licensing.

When receiving debts from different foreign countries and international organizations, in some cases the interest rate and prices on goods bought on credits were artificially increased, the credits received were used in less important directions. In this way, the foreign debt of Georgia amounted to half a billion USD. Total sum of our external debt constituted one billion USD.

Ignoring the interests of enterprise workers and employees practically hindered the privatization process in 1992-1993 and hold up the restructuring of enterprises into joint-stock companies.

All these reasons together preconditioned the energetics crisis: non-purpose-oriented use of credits, non-payments for real cost of power resources, chronic irresponsibility to observance of technical norms made it impossible to carry out not only capital, but also routine repairs; constant robbery of copper content equipment on power lines for the purpose of selling it in Turkey aggravated the situation in energetics (and not only in it). All the above-mentioned, together with energetics crisis, caused unseen decline of production.

It should also be noted that in condition of complete disorder in accounting, it became impossible to obtain a full value information on firms and their activities. Thus, in its turn, artificially reduced the generalized macroeconomic index and correspondingly the size of objects liable to taxation,

The given period of economic reform is characterized by defective registration of foreign economic relations, inactivity of customs office, squandering of commodity stocks, uncontrolled leakage of state property to foreign countries, belittling the role of legal wage, unseen expansion of shadow economy, non-targeted use of humanitarian aid.

Rebuilding the Economy

At the beginning of 1994, the Head of State of the Republic of Georgia, Mr. E. Shevardnadze initiated the elaboration of anti-crisis programs of macroeconomic stabilization and systematic changes. In spring 1994 there began practical realization of the program which made a good start to the stage of correction of errors committed during the process of economic reforms. This new period of economic reform was also characterized by problems of non-economic factors.

By spring of 1994 the hostilities had already stopped. True, it had a positive influence on economy on the whole, but there appeared a new problem: social protection of refugees and displaced people, which was a heavy burden on the budget. Up to the moment when the refugees and displaced people return to their homes the social (and not only social) problems will not be solved on the whole.

Law-enforcing institutions intensified the fight against criminals in order to improve the situation. Definite positive results have also been attained, but on the whole, unfortunately, it is still far to complete the solution of the problem. A number of enterprises do not dare to start a full load work for fear of being robbed by partially formal and other criminal elements.

From spring of 1994 the government step by step changes its attitude towards the coupon. According to a well-known ideology of the IMF it is ready to assist any country having its own currency and whose government does its best to strengthen it. If Georgia stayed within the "ruble zone" the IMF would undoubtedly prefer to work with Russia - country issuing the ruble. Such approach knocked out of those in power supporting the "ruble zone" the possibility to advocate aloud the necessity to announce the Russian ruble as legal tender and assisted those in power who, from the beginning, realized the absence of any prospect for Georgian economy without its own national currency. It must be noted here that in 1994 a hopeless, from the first sight, experiment was going on in Kutaisi and, due to the city authorities, Kutaisi appeared to be the place in Georgia where the Georgian coupon was supported by them.

All this, together with stabilization of the Georgian coupon and depreciation of the ruble intensified the tendencies of serious attitude to the coupon. Uncontrolled emission became impossible due to enviable steadfastness of the authorities of the National Bank of Georgia.

In fall of 1994 the National Bank of the Republic of Georgia canceled the restrictions on withdrawal of cash money from the banks under obvious pressure of the IMF. As a result of it cash and non-cash money values considerably drew nearer to each other. Following the recommendations of the IMF the National Bank started from the end of 1994 regulating the bank system with the help of classical methods approved in the world. Together with the solution of other problems it prevented the state-commercial banks to work in overdraft conditions. It is noteworthy, that from the second half of 1994 corporatization of the state- commercial banks has started.

According to the work out program together with the IMF in September of 1994 the price on gas and electricity have advanced to the world level, the price on bread increased 285 times, "metro" fares raised excessively and also tariffs on municipal services. There was the wage increase for those involved in budget sphere, pensions and donations were also increased, but it has considerably lagged behind the price rise. It allowed to achieve essential reduction of the budgetary subsidies for price discrepancies. It was followed by considerable strengthening of rate of the Georgian coupon. If before the price rise on bread one dollar was 5.3 million coupons, after the price rise one dollar was already 2.4 million coupons. The process continued; at the end of 1994 the price on bread increased again by 40 percent and as a result of it the stable coupon exchange rate has been fixed (one dollar equals to 1.3 million coupon), which remains immutable till now.

Unfortunately, we could not manage a full withdrawal of money not only for gas and electricity, but also for bread. If enterprises and people did not pay for gas and electricity, or paid only negligible sums, the price on bread was almost completely paid by population. The delay in timely return of these sums to the government "favored" in autumn 1994 the sceptic attitude to the coupon by economic agents: trade organizations, enterprises and banks delayed corresponding money transfer and conducted speculated operations at the currency market, thus sustaining significant losses. Starting from 1995, when the coupon rate became stable, timely withdrawal of these sums was prevented not only by sluggishness of banks, but also by some local authorities using these sums temporarily in order to settle the problems of local budget.

Pseudo protection of enterprises (so called "zombie" enterprises) by some representatives of government, and often groundless fear of the population, did not put an end, from the very beginning, to the non-payment practice by means of stoppage of delivery. Gas delivery to the population of Tbilisi stopped only in January 1995. Impossibility to collect full cost for gas and electricity did not allow the government to revise the corresponding prices. Prices in dollars an gas and electricity increased every month as a result of strengthening the coupon. It preconditioned artificial increase in the product cost having adverse affect, first of all, on industrial enterprise. On the basis of analysis of the given situation the Georgian government revised corresponding prices.

In particular, since April 1995 the cost of gas reduced to 35% and the cost of electricity to 25%. At the same time, the government of Georgia refused to purchase gas from June 1995; Its purchase had to be performed by immediate consumer, namely by "Sakenergo" (Georgian State Company of Energetics), big industrial enterprises and municipalities.

In condition to direct purchase of gas by consumers the above-mentioned Georgian clearing is practically "annulled." All this put on the agenda the necessity to annul quotation and simplify licensing. This process has already started: the system of quotation has been completely annulled since June 1, 1995, and licensing was preserved only for limited list of goods.

Definite order was established in borrowing and using debts. The foundation for this tradition was laid initially by those first debts, which Georgia received from International Monetary Fund (IMF) and the World Bank (WB).

In December 1994 Georgia received from the IMF the first tranche of Systemic Transformation Facility (STF) (approximately 39 million USD). In July, November 1994, and March 1995 Georgia received Institutional Building Loan from the World Bank (approximately 10 million USD), Rehabilitation Loan on Municipal Infrastructure (approximately 18 million USD) and Economic Rehabilitation Loan (75 million USD). STF was used by National Bank by means of purpose-oriented usage of resources to stabilize the rate of the Georgian coupon. The Institutional Building Loan is used to improve the material and technical base of government structures. As to Rehabilitation Loan it is used to finance a part of budget expenditures.

It should be noted that approval of Republican Budget by Parliament at the beginning of 1995, after a two year interval can be considered as a very important step to establish order in the financial system of Georgia. The true worth of this budget is that emission credit and emission itself were not used to balance income and expenditure. In 1995 only 47% of expenditures of Republican the Budget had to be covered by taxes and the rest 53% had to be filled up by monetarization of wheat and flour received as humanitarian aid (mobilizing proceeds of sales in the state budget). Thus, practically unbalanced budget is balanced without money emission. It is achieved with the help of donor-countries and organizations, promoting reforms in Georgia.

With the support and efforts of the IMF the majority of countries to whom Georgia's debt amounted up to approximately one billion USD, agreed to debt rescheduling. It allowed the IMF to allocate the second tranche of debt on financing the STF at the end of June 1995 (approximately 44 million USD) and the stand-by credit (approximately 113 million USD). All this will create conditions for Georgia to preserve financial stability, to carry out currency reform and to issue the Lari (national currency) in circulation so that it can be insured against errors committed by the government with respect to the coupon. The rate of national currency may remain the same till the end of 1995. If inflation rate in the first half of 1995 constituted average 2-3% a month, then in the second half of 1995 it may be average 1% a month.

It should be noted here that from July 1, 1995 minimal wage of those employed in budget sector constituted 2.69 USD and maximal 12.69 USD. It is, of course, very little, though it is not out of place to remember that at the beginning of September 1994 minimal wage was less then 10 cents, and maximal a little more than a dollar.

From the point of view of sectoral development the reforms in Georgia are carried out most intensively in health care system, where the project of the reform was elaborated in close cooperation with experts of the World Bank. In the health care sphere there is a gradual transition to paid medical service, establishing the system medical insurance. Working over the reform in the education sphere is being gradually stirred up.

In May 1994 the Head of State issued a decree according to which the enterprise personnel were given an advantage in the process of corporatization. It speeded up this process. At the same time the process of privatization, by means of direct purchases, has also been stimulated.

In Georgia in 1995 as in many post-communist countries the process of using vouchers in privatization started: a part of property is distributed to people free of charge. It is dictated by necessity of leveling of conditions when privatizing.

At a given stage the government of Georgia brisked up the work so that to attract credits into the sphere of energetics in order to overcome difficult situation. If situation in energetics is improved, and the railroad arteries through Abkhazeti and Chechnyia (Russian region) are relieved, the production will, by all means, he stirred up.

Record-keeping is gradually improving because of simplification of the system of taxation.

At a given stage of economics reform, the stability of monetary system has been achieved, considerable decline in the fall of production has stopped and in some sectors of economy there is evident growth of production. By that time all conditions will be ready to develop into the market system.

Conclusion

The Challenges facing the people and government of Georgia remain daunting. The most severe part of the economic crisis is probably surmounted, but the task of rebuilding the economy is a new shape has still to be achieved. Shortages of essential materials and skills, poor infrastructure and unproven institutions mean that for Georgia alone it would be a long process. With external assistance, however, progress could be rapid.

The strengths of Georgia lies in the high educational status of its people and the proven ability to innovate. This can potentially be translated into commercial competitiveness. The vibrance and diversity of local markets suggest that there is no lack of entrepreneurial spirit, and this should produce in time the strong institutions that will provide employment and rising incomes in the community.

Notes

1. The Georgian call themselves "Kartveli." This name goes back to the designation of the central part of East Georgia: Kartli; hence, the common term all Georgians identify themselves by: Kartveli, and habitant of Karlti. Later on, this common designation served as the basis for the name of the whole country: "Sakartvelo," Le. the land in which the Georgians live. Hence, "Kartuli ana," for example, the Georgian or the Kartvelian Language, accordingly, the study of Georgia and terms for the country and its inhabitants. The Old Persians called East Georgia "vrkana," and its population "vrk" (the etymology is vague). The Armenian term for the Georgians, "brats" is of the same origin. In the new Persian the country is called "gurgjan," and its inhabitants are know as "gurg." In Arabic-Syriac the from "djurdj," "djurzan" is used; the Turks use "gurdji" (a Georgian) and "Gurdjistan" (Georgia). This form was the basis for the Russian Terms "Gruzia, "gursin." The forms "Georgia" (Latin). "Georgie" (French). "Georgia" (English), and "Georgien" (German) wide-spread in European languages since the also 13th century, derive from the Turkish "gurji".

2. Russia's and Georgia's religion are the same: Christian Orthodox.

3. NMP (Net Material Product).

References

Beridze, T. and Silagadze, A. (1996) Status of Privatization of State owned Enterprises in the Republic of Georgia. Department of Government and Politics, University of Maryland: College Park, Maryland, USA, 1996;

Beridze, T. (1995) Transition from Command to a Market System: Correlation of Economics and Polities, Warsaw, Poland, 1995;

Beridze, T. (1995) Economic Sovereignty: New Aspects of Economics and Politics Correlation, Government Structures in the U.S. and the Sovereign States of the Former Soviet Union. Edited by James E. Hickey and Alexej Ugrinskyi. Greenwood Publishing Group, Inc: USA;

Lazear, Edward P. (1995) Economic Transition in Eastern Europe and Russia: Realities of Reform. Hoover Institution Press, Stanford University: Stanford, California, USA.

Forced Migration: Repatriation in Georgia. Open Society Institute: New York, USA;

Kaminski, Bartlomeij, Shen Kun Wang, L. Alan Winters (1995) Trade Performance Depends on Bold Reform. Transition: the Newsletter about Reforming Economies. Vol. 6, No 9-10;

Making Markets: Economies Transformation in Eastern Europe and the Post-Soviet States (1993) Edited by Shafigul Islam and Michael Mandelbaum. Council on Foreign Relations Press: New York, New York, 1993;

Murrell, Peter (1992) Privatization versus the Fresh Start: Uprooting Leninism, Cultivating Liberty. Edited by Vladimir Tismaneanu and Patrich Clawson. University Press of American, Inc: USA;

Papava, V. (1995) Georgian Economy: Main Directions and First Results of Reforms. Warsaw, Poland;

Sachs, Jeffery D. (1994) Understanding "Shock Therapy" paper for a seminar on "Post-communist Societies in Transition" at the Social Market Foundation,

June 30, 1994;

Schaffer, M. (1992) The Economy of Poland, Working Paper No. 67, March. Center for Economic Performance, London School of Economics: London, England, 1992;

Wolf, Martin (1994) Why Shock Therapy? “Financial Times”, August 4, 1994.

On the Question of Economic Growth

Abstract

Economic development looks at a wider range than GDP per capita. Economic development is concerned with how people are actually affected. It looks at their actual living standards and social conditions.

Measures of economic development will look at: Real income per head - GDP per capita; Levels of literacy and education standards; Levels of health care (for example, number of doctors per 1.000 population); Quality and availability of housing; Levels of environmental standards; Levels of infrastructure (transport, communication); Levels of corruption; Educational standards & labor productivity; Labor mobility; Flow of foreign aid & investment; Level of savings & investment; etc.

The modern world economy is a system of rather complex, closely interconnected entities (states, countries, international organizations and institutions (formal and informal), transnational corporations, individual firms, households, individuals). At the turn of the XX-XXI centuries, this system acquired a completely new quality - a global content that, in addition to its proper economy, includes politics, society, culture, religion, education, etc. These components of public life have a significant impact on the economy, and the economy in turn largely determines their content. In addition, the collapse of the socialist system and the emergence of a completely new phenomenon - transition countries, emerging economies ("transition countries, transitional economies") added new content to the process of globalization. The emergence of these countries has made more urgent the question of **how economic growth and economic development are interrelated. What is the difference between economic growth and economic development? Which indicators are used to evaluate them? Can we consider the model of economic development in the analysis of the economies of countries in transition, if it is typically only for the countries of the so-called Third World?**

The answers to the above questions require a fairly extensive and in-depth investigation. In the present article, we will only touch few areas of research (and only as the statement of questions).

Again about economic growth

The phenomenon of "economic growth" is not a new issue in economic theory and practice. From the beginning of a human economic activity, it has been in the focus of public attention for one simple reason: the economic growth is reflected in the development of the country and raising the standard of living of people, while the factors of growth are constantly present the object of research of politicians and scientists-economists. The issues of economic growth were studied by the representatives of the ideologically opposite camps of economic theory: in the XIX century - by K. Marx (the theory of reproduction, which made a significant contribution to the study of this issue) and in the twentieth century - the prominent representatives of the theory of economic growth (J. Keynes, R. Harrod, E. Domar, J. Robinson, etc.), which focused on the importance of increasing national income by considering only one factor - the rate of capital accumulation. W. Rostow links this phenomenon to the stadial development of society. Later the author of the neoclassical model of economic growth J. Meade focuses on all its factors (capital, savings, labor, investments) and believes that only in this case the economic growth will be stable and sustainable.

All researchers of this problem try to answer the questions: what is economic growth? What determines economic growth and how is it measured? It is well known that all these questions are answered in the textbooks of macroeconomics[1], but in our opinion, a certain circle of questions remains that needs to be explained and developed.

It is well known that economists mainly measure economic growth by the dynamics of Gross Domestic Product (GDP). However, we note that this figure does not fully reflect economic growth, as it does not show the quality of life of the country and the effect of distributional relations, but also includes the volume of financial intermediation operations, which do not reflect the growth of the economy in the real sector. Given these circumstances, economists use other indicators as well - gross national income; net national income; personal income; net personal income, or disposable income. **The social components of gross domestic product creation should also be considered**.

What determines the growth of the gross domestic product? The answer is simple at first glance: the level of productivity in the country (it must be said

[1] Karl E. Case, Ray C. Fair. Principles of Economics. Eighth Edition. Pearson Prentice Hall. 2007. P.543-698. J. Kakhniashvili. Macroeconomics. Tbilisi, publ. house “Siakhle”, 1996, pp. 210-277 (in Georgian) etc.

that for the last two decades this figure has not been calculated by statistical bodies at all). What are its determinants? These are **physical capital** (equipment and buildings used to produce goods and services), **human capital** (knowledge and skills that a person acquires through education and practical experience), **natural resources** (materials used in the production of goods and services, provided by nature), **technological knowledge** (introduction of the state-of-the-art technology and "know-how"). This factor is gaining special importance in the modern economy (this factor is extremely important for Georgia and therefore the government's policy should be aimed at importing technologies). We also note that during the last 25 years, the production base of the Georgian economy has not been renewed and it is really difficult to talk about the growth of the industrial base, which is the basis for the growth of all other sectors.

All factors of production contribute to economic growth, but, naturally, not equally (not everyone has the same weight), since any country has the advantage of using this or that factor, which gives it advantages in foreign trade. Naturally, the more optimal the combination of these factors, the higher the economic growth and its stability (in the Soviet period the economists-mathematicians even developed the so-called **system of optimal functioning of the economy**).

What is the situation in modern Georgia in this regard? Unfortunately, it should be noted that in the last 20-25 years, all these determinants (factors) in Georgia are practically are more and more worsening! The focus is on one or two industries, whereas the focus should be on the optimal sector structure. The answer is not simple, perhaps the model should be used here - costs-output and also many socio-economic indicators.

Let's take **physical capital**. It is mostly worn out, it is not replaced or re-equipped (which usually has to be done every 20-25 years), whereas industrial machinery and production lines are the basis of modern economics. The country's import policy should be reviewed from this point of view. The consumer economy model must be refused.

As for **human capital** - more than a million people (mostly aged 25-50) have left the country, and education (especially engineering) is in poor condition. The system of professions and specialties and the training of specialists should also be reviewed taking into account the interests of the country.

Natural resources - the ecological equilibrium in the country is disturbed (there are no statistics on the ecological equilibrium), while the ecosystem is an important component of the socio-economic system and contributes not only to public health but also to economic growth.

As for the double-digit growth of GDP (in 1996-1997 and 2004), it was caused only by the so-called **effect of sharp growth** (in the terminology of Gregory Mankiw) and the **recovery of the economy** (in the terminology of the Russian economist E. Gaidar).

The economic policy of the country must be developed in these circumstances.

The essence and indicators of economic development

Economic development is a relatively new concept and is much broader than economic growth. It is reflected in textbooks and is taught in many higher education institutions[2] around the world. Therefore, first of all, it is important to perceive differences between economic growth and economic development. At first glance, posing the issue in this way is a tautology, but in a more in-depth study, we will see the fundamental differences between them, which are due to the difference between the technical-economic and socio-economic aspects of the economy. The first focuses on the development of the economy in terms of developing its productive potential, while the second is focused on the social consequences of economic development. In this sense, the model of economic development is, to some extent, a continuation of the "socially-oriented economic" model established in West Germany and the Scandinavian countries since the second half of the twentieth century.

It is well known that economic growth is measured in terms of the real output of GDP (including GDP per capita), while economic development is much broader than economic growth. It is more socially oriented and reflects many layers of the country's development.

Economic development shows the direct effect of economic growth on the population, how the standard of living in the country increases, and therefore it is measured by such indicators as a real income (GDP) per capita; the level of education; the level of health (for example, number of doctors per 1000 people); protection of ecological standards. At the same time, the economic development is significantly determined by the level of infrastructure (transport, communications); efficiency of the service sector[3]; low level of corruption; labor productivity; workforce mobility; a flow of foreign investment and aid; level of

[2] Hayami Y. and Godo Y. Development Economics. From the Poverty to the Wealth of Nations. Third Edition. 2002

[3] In this regard, it is necessary to mention the monographic research of R. Asatiani "Service and market system, Tbilisi, "Tbilisi University Publisher, 1993 (in Georgian)

savings and investments, etc.

Let us now consider what economic growth can be like without development.

1. **The effects of economic growth are reflected in the well-being of only a small number of people**. For example, in an oil-rich country, GDP is growing. In this case, the firm's income may increase dramatically, but this does not necessarily mean that this wealth is equally reflected in the entire population;

2. **Corruption.** The country may have high levels of GDP, but the effect of its growth will be reflected only in the bank accounts of oligarchs and politicians. The question of how to measure the level of corruption in Georgia is relevant. Legal statistics provide only dry statistics on corruption crimes, but this is only one side of the coin, much more relevant is the question of how corruption harms the country, in particular, the budget-tax system[4];

3. **Environmental problems**. Production of toxic chemical products (and other harmful products) increases GDP, but improper regulation of their production can harm the environment and health, making it much more expensive for society, and the country as a whole;

4. **Overloading of the economy**. Focusing only on the technical-economic side of economic growth can lead to a waste of resources in the economy, which is also unacceptable for sustainable development;

5. **Improper level of use of manufactured products**. At first glance, this may sound paradoxical, but it is a very topical issue and is related, on the one hand, to the efficiency of distributional relations and, on the other hand, to the inadequate distribution (allocation) of resources;

6. **Expenditure on armaments**. Planning and incurring optimal budget expenditure is important for the country's development (this has been very important for Georgia in recent years, as rising expenditure on armaments has significantly reduced social expenses).

Finally, let us try to answer the question: Can the model of economic development be used in the analysis of transitional (post-communist) economies or for their future development?

The use of this model at the present stage is appropriate in the sense that the economic reforms of the past years have disrupted the social orientation of the country and aimed only at technical-economic growth. Therefore it is necessary to use this indicator. The economic policy of Georgia should be aimed at overcoming the existing economic lag.

---

[4] K. Shevardnadze, R. Chechelashvili, V. Chocheli, N. Khaduri. Papava Indexes of Tax Corruption. Tbilisi. "Company Imperial Ltd" Publisher, 2000

On the Question of Transitional Period in Economy

Abstract

The article deals with the topical issues of the theory and methodology of transitional economy. There is found the necessity of developing the theory of transitional economy and indicators reflecting the development of the transition period. Special attention is paid to the issue of ownership and management in transitional period and the need of vision of the results of the transitional period in economy.

Today, two decades after the beginning of the so-called “transitional period” from a command economy to a market economy, in a society of countries (and there are 26 of them with almost 300 million population, without of China), who have made such a transition, legitimate questions arise about the correctness and effectiveness of the taken steps. In this integrated world post-communist countries will play a **key role in economics, politics, culture and social life.** Therefore, there is a need for an objective assessment of what we have received as a result of this socio-economic transformation in the post-Soviet space. It should be recognized that ***there is an objective need to develop a “theory of a transitional economy.”*** Today, the development of such a theory with its importance can be compared with the development in its time of the basic theories of economic science.

The economy of the transitional period has a number of specific characteristics that differ from economies in a stationary state and developing on their own basis. In particular, in the transitional economy, newly emerging institutions replace connections and relations of the old ones. As a result, new macro- and microeconomic patterns and trends, social and political changes, a new content of economic policy are emerging.

There was also an economic scientific discipline (**transitology**) the subject of which is the problem of economic transformation, and the **object** – the economy of a country or countries in the process of transition from one state of the socio-economic system to a qualitatively different state. For obvious historical reasons, the focus of scientists-transitologists (the term “transitology” was proposed in 1992 by Michael Buravoi deals with the transition from a centrally planned socialist economy to a capitalist market economy, considered in close connection with political, socio-cultural and other aspects.

Actually, the problems of the transitional period were still posed at the beginning of the 20th century in the works of the Marxist trend – K.Kautsky "On the Day after the Proletarian Revolution," N. Bukharin "Economy of the Transition Period." However, these works had two drawbacks: the problems of transition were interpreted in them in a straightforward manner and, in fact, were reduced to an analysis of only the problems of the transition from capitalism to socialism.

The practice itself "gave birth" to various theoretical and methodological approaches to transformational processes, which ultimately come down to two major trends, schools: this gradual, "gradualist" (from the English word "gradual") transition to the market (more cautious and piecemeal approach to reforms), and the transition to a market in forced mode – the so-called "shock therapy,"(radical reforms and rapid transformation) or simply the set of specific steps, postulates developed in 1989 by the International Monetary Fund (IMF), the World Bank and the US Treasury for Latin American countries and referred to as the "Washington Consensus:"

According to the author of this consensus, John Williamson, he included 10 steps by governments: ***strengthening of financial discipline, revising the priorities for the distribution of public wealth in favor of the poor, tax reform, interest rate liberalization, the introduction of a more flexible exchange rate, liberalization of foreign trade, investment, privatization, deregulation, maintenance of property rights.***

Over the years, the UN General Assembly has debated country classification issues. For example, in 1971 the General Assembly identified a group of Least Developed Countries to be afforded special attention in the context of implementing the second UN Development Decade for the 1970s. Follow-up UN conferences have monitored progress in addressing the development challenges in these countries. However, the General Assembly has never established a development taxonomy for its full membership. In contrast, international organizations have established such taxonomies, and in this section the development taxonomies used by three such organizations—the UNDP, the World Bank, and the IMF—are explored.

The UNDP's country classification system is built around the Human Development Index (HDI) launched together with the Human Development Report (HDR) in 1990. To capture the multifaceted nature of development, the HDI is a composite index of three indices measuring countries' achievements in longevity, education, and income. Other aspects of development—such as political freedom and personal security—were also recognized as important, but the lack of data prevented their inclusion into the HDI. Over the years, the index has been refined, but the index's basic structure has not changed. In the HDR 2010, the income measure used in the HDI is Gross National Income per capita (GNI/n) with local currency estimates converted into equivalent US dollars using Purchasing Power Parity (PPP). Longevity is measured by life expectancy at birth. For education, a proxy is constructed by combining measures of actual and expected years of schooling. Measures of achievements in the three dimensions do not enter directly into the sub-indices, but undergo a transformation.

The problem of the "transition period" in the economy, strange as it sounds, is also old, if we mean, say, the transitional state of the 1920's in the USSR, or transitional periods of social development in the countries of industrial development, or transitional periods of social development in the countries of industrial development, where the level of industrial development was the cornerstone of the periodization of the development of socio-economic systems, and the new one, if we mean the last decade of the 20th century and the beginning of the 21st century, marked by a transition from planned, centrally regulated economy to an economy based on market principles.

"Transitional state" in the natural sciences is one thing, and in the social sciences it is fundamentally different, since the essential point of the latter is precisely social relations, relations between people.

In our analysis, we confine ourselves to the **question** of methodological approaches to the study of the phenomenon of the transitional economy. These are such principles as: a) the complexity, the integrity of the study of the transitional economy; b) disclosure of the very content of the transitional economy, its structure; c) its quantification; d) vision of the final results of this process.

First of all, a terminological definiteness should be established regarding the phenomenon of "transitional economy." Two terms are used in Western economic literature – "transitional economy" and "emerging markets;" in the latter, in addition to the transition countries there are included also the countries of the so-called "third world."

The concept of "transition," "transitional period," "transitional state" should be defined. In social science it is somewhat conditional. "The transition from what?" "Transition to what?" What is the content and quantitative aspect of the "transition?" When does the "transition" begin? When does the "transition" end? What is the specificity of the "transition" in the economy and in society as a whole? These processes should proceed in synchronous mode or at different rates?

If, under the transition is understood as a change in the form of ownership (in this case, public to private), then it is necessary to see the difference between the legal and economic content of property relations. In the first case, the main content is the ownership of the property object to the subject (what to whom) - the state, an individual, a group of persons (here we recall the postulate in the famous "Coase theorem": it is not so important how the property is distributed, it is important that the property rights are clearly fixed), in the second case – in economic one, the main content is the effectiveness of the use of this property **(which is how)**. In other words, the form of affiliation is important for a lawyer and its content for an economist. In other words, ***for a lawyer the form of ownership is important, and for an economist – its content.*** That is why privatization, which is the main means and form of property change, should not become an end in itself in the transition to the market, but only its tool – an instrument in the creation of an effective owner.

Following the logic of compulsory separation of the core in property relations, it is necessary to recognize that the ***dominant*** form in property relations in the transition economy (along with others) are private property relations laying the foundations for future economies.

An important issue of the content of the transitional economy and society is its social structure. After all, new property relations give rise to a new social structure. The class approach to its content proposed in the past is well known and was largely a reflection of past relationships. ***The issue of the difference between the social structure of the transitional society and the social structure of the already formed modern market economy is also relevant here.*** The social structure of the transitional society represents the interaction of the subjects of the old system of relations and the subjects of the emerging system of relations. Despite the fact that these subjects are the product of economic relations, their transformation is much more complex than the transformation of purely economic forms.

Among the issues related to the substantive side of the development of the transitional economy should be highlighted the problem around which revolve all other issues, and such a problem, in our opinion, is the ***awareness of the role of the state in the economy in general, and particularly in transitional one***. Today, there are no countries with absolutely market economy (without state meddling) anywhere (except in textbooks on macroeconomics), market economy, in our opinion, a priori and immanently implies the participation of the state in economic processes. This has been demonstrated by the current economic and financial crisis in the world, the overcoming of which is sought in the bowels of governmental structures of the state and international economic and financial organizations. The question arises: where is the market automatism of the way-out of the crisis? It simply does not exist, and cannot be due to the immanent properties of the market.

The principal issue in the transition countries is the way to manage their societies and the state. Immediately at the beginning of the transitional period, a policy of democratization of society and the political system was proclaimed, without taking into account the traditions and mentality of the population. In almost all countries in transition, democracy has been proclaimed as a way of governing society and the state. But unfortunately, we must admit ***that in almost many transitional countries we have received a formal democracy (or substantive democracy is a form in which the outcome of elections is representative of the people. In other words, substantive democracy is a form of democracy that functions in the interest of the governed) and a parliamentary system as a way of coming to power and retaining it.***

In our view, the most correct assessment of the adequacy of the transition period is its quantitative assessment, which will make it possible to judge the success of the process, its time frame and content. Ultimately, it is a question of assessing the effectiveness of economic policies in the transition process. What indicators can reflect the success or failure of the transitional period in the economy?

In general, the problem of indicators has different aspects: indicators can be techno-economic (financial-general), material and socio-economic. The first is the quantitative changes in production and its results (production of products per unit of labor). Then there are the production indicators of technological or power equipment. There are indicators of development costs, primarily investments in production. There are indicators of results, for example, for the most important types of products (steel, aluminum, grain, etc.). Finally, indicators are reflecting the overall result.

An independent, an important "section" of the indicators of the economic performance of the society are socio-economic indicators: availability of jobs, the level of personal (family) consumption of goods, the level of cash income (and wages), housing, income stratification, the level of poverty (below the minimum subsistence level, the level of survival), the degree of intensity of work, the availability and amount of free time, the level of education, etc.

Graph 1 - **Unemployment rate in Georgia (%) 2006-2017**

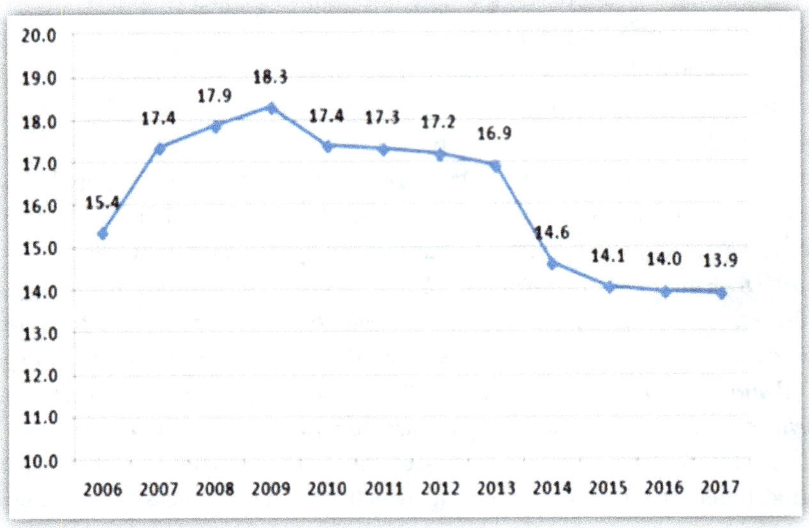

Source: National Statistics office of Georgia
http://www.geostat.ge/?action=page&p_id=145&lang=geo

In graph 1 there is shown that in 2017 the unemployment rate in Georgia decreased by 0.1 percentage points compared to 2016 and equaled 13.9 percent. It should be noted that the downtrend in the unemployment rate is maintained during the last eight years. In 2017 the economically active population constituted 65.8 percent of the working population (population of 15 years and older). Compared to 2016 the economic activity rate and employment rate decreased by 0.5 and 0.4 percentage points, respectively. The employment rate in urban settlements decreased by 1.5 percentage point compared to the previous year, while increasing by 0.8 percentage points in rural areas. Similarly, compared to the previous year the economic activity rate in the urban settlements decreased by 1.6 percentage points and increased by 0.8 percentage points in rural areas.

Graph 2 **- Poverty Level in Georgia (%) 2006-2017**

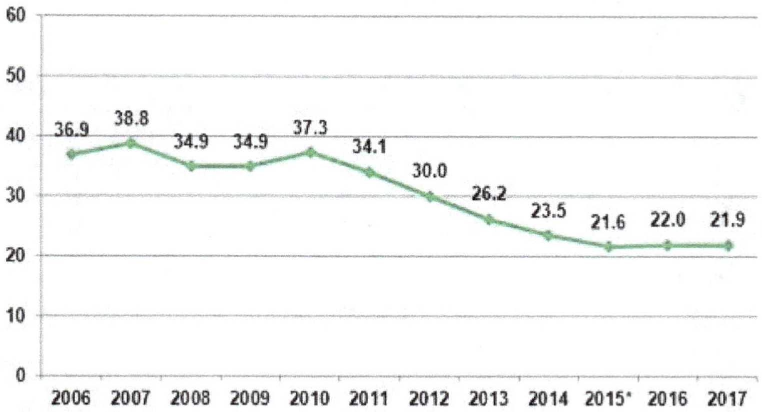

Source: National Statistics office of Georgia
http://www.geostat.ge/?action=page&p_id=145&lang=geo

Graph 2 shows the share of population under absolute poverty line by percentage in 2006-2017 in Georgia, which is 21.9% according to the recent indicator, which is increased by 0.9 percentage points compared to the previous year.

It is not about the systematic of indicators, but it is important to emphasize that ***the result of the economic activity of society cannot be expressed by any one indicator, but rather assumes a systematic approach within the overall context of the study.***

Today, the number of indicators reflecting the functioning of enterprises (firms, companies) is reduced to a minimum, practically operate only with profit at the micro level, and GDP at the macro level.

If we take the macro level, we note that the value of GDP is affected by fictitious capital, which occupies a large place in developed market economies. In General, GDP is not the gross product itself, but rather an uncertain amount of money "contribution" of any branches of labor activity (if you take a Bank, an insurance company, a money-changing office, a service office, etc.) for labor activity. The more such units are the higher the GDP is. GDP is a consolidated financial indicator that can say something (not all) about the dynamics of a single country and then only when involving in the analysis of many data, in particular the share of production in GDP. The high GDP per capita still says little about a country's position in the "world economy." The volume of exports (per capita) is also of no independent importance.

Table 1 **– GDP in the countries with the transitional economies**

Economies in transition: rates of growth of real GDP, 2009–2019

Annual percentage change

	2009–2016[a]	2009	2010	2011	2012	2013	2014	2015	2016	2017[b]	2018[c]	2019[c]
Economies in transition	0.9	-6.6	4.8	4.6	3.4	2.4	0.9	-2.2	0.4	2.2	2.3	2.4
South-Eastern Europe	1.0	-2.0	1.5	1.7	-0.7	2.4	0.2	2.0	2.9	2.5	3.2	3.3
Albania	2.5	3.4	3.7	2.5	1.4	1.1	2.0	2.6	3.5	3.8	3.8	3.7
Bosnia and Herzegovina	0.9	-2.9	0.8	0.9	-0.9	2.4	1.1	3.1	3.0	3.0	3.0	3.0
Montenegro	1.1	-5.7	2.5	3.2	-2.7	3.5	1.8	3.4	2.9	4.0	3.8	3.5
Serbia	0.2	-3.1	0.6	1.4	-1.0	2.6	-1.8	0.7	2.8	2.0	3.0	3.3
The former Yugoslav Republic of Macedonia	2.2	-0.4	3.4	2.3	-0.5	2.9	3.6	3.8	2.4	1.6	3.0	3.3
Commonwealth of Independent States and Georgia[d]	0.9	-6.8	4.9	4.7	3.6	2.4	1.0	-2.4	0.3	2.2	2.3	2.4
Commonwealth of Independent States and Georgia - net fuel exporters	1.1	-6.3	4.9	4.6	3.9	2.5	1.4	-1.9	0.2	2.2	2.2	2.2
Azerbaijan	2.5	9.4	4.6	-1.6	2.1	5.9	2.7	0.7	-3.1	-1.0	1.8	2.3
Kazakhstan	4.1	1.2	7.3	7.4	4.8	6.0	4.2	1.2	0.9	4.0	3.0	3.0
Russian Federation	0.4	-7.8	4.5	4.3	3.7	1.8	0.7	-2.8	-0.2	1.8	1.9	1.9
Turkmenistan	9.3	6.1	9.2	14.7	11.1	10.2	10.3	6.5	6.2	6.0	4.8	5.0
Uzbekistan	8.1	8.1	8.5	8.3	8.2	8.0	8.1	7.9	7.8	6.5	6.4	6.1
Commonwealth of Independent States and Georgia - net fuel importers	-0.8	-10.5	5.0	5.5	1.3	1.2	-2.6	-6.0	1.2	2.4	2.8	3.5
Armenia	1.0	-14.1	2.2	4.7	7.2	3.3	3.6	3.0	0.2	5.8	3.8	3.6
Belarus	1.4	0.2	7.7	5.5	1.7	1.0	1.7	-3.9	-2.7	1.5	2.0	2.3
Georgia[d]	3.7	-3.7	6.2	7.2	6.4	3.4	4.6	2.9	2.7	4.8	4.3	4.3
Kyrgyzstan	3.8	2.9	-0.5	6.0	-0.1	10.5	4.3	3.5	3.8	6.1	5.8	4.7
Republic of Moldova	3.0	-6.0	7.1	6.8	-0.7	9.4	4.8	-0.7	4.3	3.2	4.0	4.0
Tajikistan	5.7	4.0	6.5	2.4	7.5	7.4	6.7	4.2	6.9	5.5	6.0	6.0
Ukraine[e]	-2.7	-15.1	4.1	5.4	0.2	0.0	-6.6	-9.9	2.2	1.8	2.5	3.6

Source: UN/DESA, based on data of the United Nations Statistics Division and individual national sources.

Note: Regional aggregates calculated at 2010 prices and exchange rates.

a) Average percentage change.
b) b Partly estimated.
c) c Baseline scenario forecasts, based in part on Project LINK and the UN/DESA World Economic Forecasting Model.
d) d Georgia officially left the Commonwealth of Independent States on 18 August 2009. However, its performance is discussed in the context of this group of countries for reasons of geographic proximity and similarities in economic structure.

e) Starting in 2010, data for the Ukraine excludes the temporarily occupied territory of the Autonomous Republic of Crimea and Sevastopol.

Table 2 **- Gross Domestic Product (GDP), Georgia 2010-2018**

	2010	2011	2012	2013	2014	2015	2016	2017*	I 18*	II 18*
GDP at current prices, mil. GEL	20743.4	24344.0	26167.3	26847.4	29150.5	31755.6	34028.5	38042.2	9150.2	10168.4
GDP at constant 2010 prices, mil. GEL	20743.4	22241.4	23653.8	24454.9	25585.6	26322.5	27072.4	28422.3	6323.3	7239.6

Source: National Statistics office of Georgia
http://www.geostat.ge/?action=page&p_id=145&lang=geo

Table 2 describes that in Q2 2018 the real growth rate of Gross Domestic Product (GDP) amounted to 5.5 percent year-on-year, while the GDP deflator increased by 4.8 percent. The nominal GDP totaled GEL 10 168.4 million. The real GDP growth amounted to 5.4 percent for the first half of 2018.

In the following Diagram there is shown the GDP structure by the Q2 in 2018 in Georgia. Real growth was registered in the following activities: Financial Intermediation (22.0 percent), Other Community, Social and Personal Service activities (17.9 percent), Real Estate, Renting and Business Activities (13.8 percent), Wholesale and Retail Trade; Repair of Motor Vehicles, Motorcycles and Personal and Household Goods (10.5 percent), Manufacturing (8.5 percent), Mining and Quarrying (8.1 percent), Transport (8.0 percent), Education (4.8 percent), Hotels and Restaurants (4.5 percent), A decrease in the real value-added occurred in Construction (-7.1 percent), Agriculture, Hunting and Forestry; Fishing (-3.3 percent).

The largest shares of GDP by activity are held by Industry (17.1 percent) and Trade services (17.0 percent), followed by Transport and Communication (9.9 percent), Agriculture, Hunting and Forestry; Fishing (8.5 percent), Construction (8.3 percent), Public administration (7.9 percent) Real Estate, Renting and Business Activities (6.7 percent), Health and Social work (5.9 percent).

Diagram 1 – **Gross Domestic Product (GDP) by sectors in Georgia Q2 in 2018**

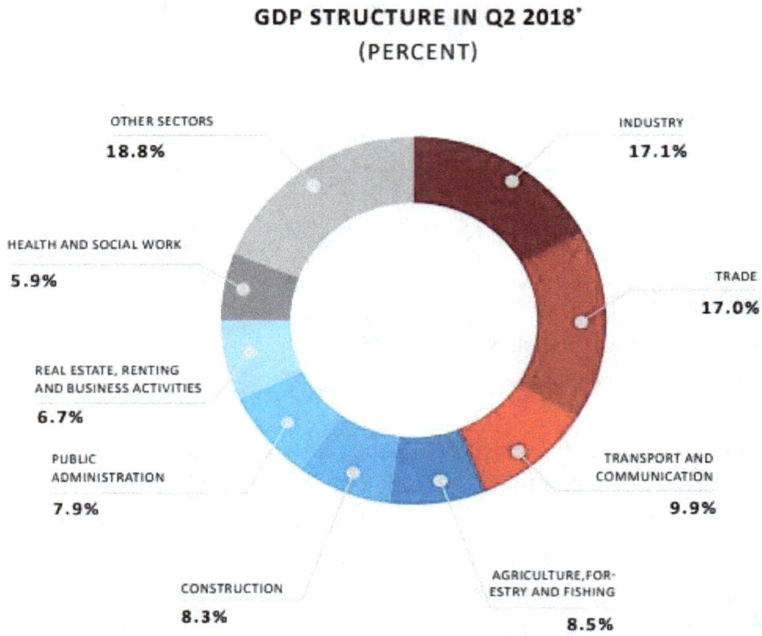

Source: National Statistics office of Georgia
http://www.geostat.ge/?action=page&p_id=145&lang=geo

If we take the micro-level, it should be recognized that the focus only on profit does not reflect all aspects of the functioning of enterprises, for example, does not take into account the technical-economic and technical side of the efficiency of the enterprise, etc. The Current situation at the micro-level of the economy in the transitional countries once again confirms the importance and need for internal planning, and this requires a whole system of indicators reflecting the level of efficiency of the enterprise.

What will we get after the "transitional" economy or more correctly, what should we get as a result of the "transitional economy" and what we have received today? Here you cannot limit yourself to economic results, but should see the result as a whole, in all its manifestations (political, socio - cultural, moral, etc.).

From the point of view of the economy, the result should be the formation of a market economy with all its attributes and institutions. Here we note that there is no constantly functioning market economy (as well as any other economy) due, first of all, to its cyclical nature of development and the action of its fundamental principle – supply and demand. After all, at least bringing demand and supply into balance needs a certain time and during this time the economy cannot be as effective as possible; secondly, the transitional economy is added to the objective circumstances of the transition difficulties: political, economic, social, cultural, etc.; thirdly, the factor of action of the subjective factor is also important, which can negate even properly developed solutions.

What should be the result of the transitional economy? This economy should be fundamentally different from the economy of the capitalist type characteristic of the second half of the 20th century. ***It should be a post-industrial type,*** taking into account the new, fifth technological structure (1985 – 2035), and given the limited resources in the world economy, the following tasks will come to the fore: a) long-term increase in resource productivity; b) solving energy problems; c) fair distribution of income. The fifth way: information and communication technologies, microelectronics, software, automation and telecommunication equipment. The sixth way – the use of the sphere of human thought (no-sphere) or biocomputer, compatible with the human mind (intelligence).

The point of view of Professor Gavriil Popov is interesting in this respect: "Capitalism could never defeat socialism. Socialism was a more progressive system than capitalism, and could only be defeated by an even higher system, which is often called ***post-industrial.***"

What do we have for today? Despite the universal nature of the tools of transition to a market economy, different results are obtained in different countries. In the countries of Central and Eastern Europe this is one thing (relatively high economic growth), in the territory of the former USSR it is another (lack of vision of the final results of reforms), in the case of China - the third (the old political system and new economic relations, and unprecedented economic growth, though recently somewhat slowed). Regarding Georgia, let us say that today the economy of Georgia is given at the mercy of the actions of natural factors, and all this is done under the slogan of protecting liberalism in the economy and democratic values in general, thereby downplaying the very idea and the possibility of a normal market economy. And in the "system" of the estimated indicators of the socio-economic development of the country, ratings of all kinds have become the main element.

And the last thing. There is always the danger that as a result of the transitional period in society and the economy, we can get a type of society, a state that may be on the margins of economic and historical progress, and whose function will be to implement the complementary tasks facing industrialized countries. And in order to avoid this, a huge responsibility lies with the governments of the countries that once were a part of the socialist system.

References:

1. The Radiant Past: Ideology and Reality in Hungary's Road to Capitalism (1992) Chicago University Press. (with Janos Lukas);
2. Economics as a science: understanding its procedures and the irrelevance of prediction. Adam Fforde. Victoria University, Australia. Real World economic review. Issue no. 81;
3. Stability, Security and sovereignty in the Republic of Georgia. David l. Philips Senior Fellow and Deputy Director. Centre for Preventive Action. Council on Foreign Relations. 8 January 2004;
4. Transformations **of the State?** Edited by Stephan Leibfried and Michael Zum. Cambridge University Press. Published in the United States of America by Cambridge University Press, New York;
5. The Economic Times. https://economictimes.indiatimes.com/news/economy/indicators/world-bank-to-change-classification-of-countries-india-will-now-be-called-lower-middle-income/articleshow/52512636.cms
6. Williamson John (1990) Latin American Adjustment: How Much Has Happened;
7. World Economic Situation and Prospects 2018, UN, https://www.un.org/development/desa/dpad/wp-content/uploads/sites/45/publication/WESP2018_Full_Web-1.pdf
8. Papava V., (1996a) The Georgian Economy: From "Shock Therapy" to "Social Promotion." *Communist Economies & Economic Transformation,* Vol. 8, No;
9. Papava V., (1996b) "Social Promotion" of Economic Reform in Georgia. *Economic Systems,* Vol. 20, No.4;
10. Papava V., (1999) The Georgian Economy: Main Directions and Initial Results of Reforms. In: *Systemic Change in Post-Communist Economies.* Selected Papers from the Fifth World Congress of Central and

East European Studies, Warsaw, 1995. Ed. by P. G. Hare. London, Macmillan Press;

11. Papava V., (2002) Necroeconomics – the Theory of Post-Communist Transformation of an Economy. *International Journal of Social Economics*, Vol. 29, No. 9-1;
12. Papava V., (2005a) *Necroeconomics: The Political Economy of Post-Communist Capitalism*. New York, iUniverse.
13. Papava V., (2005b) On the Theory of Post-Communist Economic Transition to Market. *International Journal of Social Economics*, Vol. 32, No. 1/2.
14. Papava V., (2012) Economic Reforms in Post-Communist Georgia: Twenty Years After. New York, Nova Science Publishers.
15. Беридзе Т., (1995) *Экономические основы суверенитета: новые аспекты взаимодействия экономики и политики.* Тбилиси, «Мецниереба», «Сиахле»;
16. Папава В., (1992) О приватизации основных факторов производства. *Правила игры. Fair Play*, № 3;
17. Папава В., Беридзе Т., (2005) *Очерки политической экономии посткоммунистического капитализма (опыт Грузии).* Москва, «Дело и Сервис»;
18. Меквабишвили Э., (1998) О противоречиях переходной экономики. *Общество и экономика*, № 2;
19. Силагадзе А., (1998) Социально-экономические аспекты приватизации государственного имущества в Грузии. *Общество и экономика*, № 2;
20. Блауг М. „Методология экономической науки, или Как экономисты объясняют". М.: НП „Редакция журнала Вопросы экономики". 2004.- 416 с.;
21. И.А. Болдырев Экономическая методология сегодня: краткий обзор основных направлений/Проблемы экономической теории//Журнал Новой экономической ассоциации. 2011. №9. с.47-70;
22. Бухарин Н.И. Экономика переходного периода/ч. 1. Общая теория трасформационного процесса/ Николай Бухарин. М.:Гос. Издательство, 1920. -157 с.;
23. Е.Гайдар. Восстановительный рост и некоторые особенности современной экономической ситуации в России// Вопросы экономики. #5. 1992;
24. www.geostat.ge

25. https://en.wikipedia.org/wiki/Substantive_democracy.

The National Economic Model and Globalization (The Case of Georgia)

The question formulated in the title of this article became a focus of social studies in the late 20" and early 21 centuries 1), which was due, in the first place, to the disintegration of the bipolar world and the emergence of new sovereign states (CIS, Eastern Europe). Their natural response was a desire, on the one hand, to create new "independent" economic systems and, on the other, to enter the world economic sphere. Initially, this desire appeared to be contradictory, because integration into the world economy Implied the need to "surrender" (in some measure) their economic sovereignty 2). But it should be noted that economic sovereignty is always relative ("economic independence" in the strict sense of the term is utterly unrealistic), because otherwise it implies a closed (oriented toward maximum self-sufficiency) and, consequently, inefficient economic system. The degree of relativity of economic sovereignty is higher than that of political sovereignty, which follows from the very phenomenon of economic relations (satisfaction of material needs based on a division of labor and an exchange of its results), and also from the specific nature of human economic activity implying a removal of national state barriers and the creation of a nationwide and then a worldwide market. This suggests that unity (a contradictory unity) of the international and the national is something of a norm to which economic development "tends." At the same time, the absence or weakness of one of these factors is a symptom of an incomplete or uneven realization of the overall economic potential.

1) See, for example: J. Stiglitz, Globalization and its Discontents, W.W. Norton, New York, 2002.

2) The problem of economic sovereignty was examined in: T.A. Beridze, Economic grounds of Sovereignty: new aspects of economics and politics interaction, "Novelty" Publishers, Tbilisi, 1995; A fruitful analysis of this problem is given in: H. Hinsley, Sovereignty, 2nd ed., Cambridge University Press, Cambridge, 1986; J.H. Franklin, "Sovereignty and the Mixed Constitution," in: The Cambridge History of Political Thought, 1450-1700, ed. by J.H. Burns, Cambridge University Press, Cambridge, 1991, pp. 309-328.

Assessing Georgia's current socio-economic developments is not an easy task: the aspects are varied (politics, economics, society, religion), while the period was far from easy (elections added political and economic tension). This is a strict confirmation that the economy and politics are intertwined and that their interaction plays an important role in public life.

Regarding the Definition of "National Economic Model"

The concept of "national" is used here as an attribute feature of a state entity, in contrast to "national' as an inherent attribute of a certain ethnos. In the latter case, one can only speak of national sovereignty where the actor is a nation (ethnos). A confusion of the concepts of "state" and "national" or their identification can have negative consequences. The trends observed in the territory of the former Soviet Union (Azerbaijan, Georgia, Moldova) are a good example of such confusion.

As regards the concept of "model," its most general definition is a simplified system used to simulate some aspects of the real economy 3). More specifically, one can say that an economic model (paradigm) is a certain mode of organization of socioeconomic life, a type of relationship between economic agents in the production, distribution, exchange and consumption of goods and services.

A general requirement here is that an economic model of society should ensure sustainable economic growth and, as a consequence, reduce unemployment and inflation rates, as well as ensure appropriate distribution of income.

The concept of "national" used in reference to "economic model" implies, in the first place, effective use of absolute (to a lesser extent) and relative (to a greater extent) advantages in the course of economic activity.

These priorities are conditioned by a number of factors, such as the availability of natural and human resources, a convenient geo-economic position (Azerbaijan and Georgia are good examples), etc.

A "national economic model" is a reflection of the natural form of the state's economic existence, since it underlies "relative" economic independence (absolute economic independence does not exist), given that economic sovereignty is always relative and implies, first and foremost, independence in making and implementing decisions.

3) See. J. Black, A Dictionary of Economics, Second Edition, Oxford University Press. Oxford, New York, 2002. 5 See: T.A. Beridze, op. cit., pp. 24-25.

When speaking of a "national economic model," we do not mean a "model" reflecting the content, the very type of organization of the "producer-consumer relationship (market or non-market), but the peculiarities (a number of distinctive features) of a given country's development. No "model" can be conceived or, most importantly, implemented in practice unless these peculiarities are taken into account.

What kind of economic development "model" can be chosen by the states of the Central Caucasus? Clearly, this question is not a simple one. The answer to it, in our opinion, could be as follows: first, organization of the economy according to market principles; second, reorientation of its structure in accordance with the existing realities (world market conditions, technical and technological ties); and third, due regard for traditions and other noneconomic circumstances.

Here we want to raise the question of "small countries"/ "small economies". According to the political point of view there are no "small" and "big countries"; International law gives us a theoretical basis for such an assertion. But according to the economic point of view we can talk about small economies". What is to be understood as "small economy: Territory? Population? Gross Domestic Product (GDP)? GDP per capita? A positive balance of payments? Or something else? It is not an easy question, because it is composed of many indicators. The composite indicator construction was created and adopted by the United Nations (UN): GDP per capita, longevity and education. Still, I think that this question is still open and thus deserves the continuation of the study. At any rate, this composite indicator must include economic (technical) and social aspects, and not include some demo-geographic aspects.

As regards the first factor, everything appears to be quite clear, just as the basic principles of organizing a market-based society, although the experience of the Central Caucasian countries gained in the course of market reforms shows that a number of mistakes have been committed in the process of this transition" 4).

The second factor reorientation of the economic structure is, on the one hand, a result of the operation of the first factor and, on the other, a part of current practical politics with all its pluses and minuses.

4) See, for example: Vladimer Papava, International Monetary Fund in Georgia: achievements and errors," “Imperial Publishers”, Tbilisi, 2001.

What is the structural composition of the Central Caucasus economies? Despite the region's small area, one cannot say that the structures of these economies are of the same type. In the case of Azerbaijan, it is an orientation toward energy resources and Industry, in the case of Georgia, it is agriculture, small-scale industry, transport, communications and tourism; and in the case of Armenia, it is agriculture and small- scale industry. One can say that all of this is the structural effect of these countries, which should be both the cause and the consequence of the operation of in their economies; it should underlie the construction and implementation of a "national economic model."

Strictly speaking, the "structural effect" concept needs to be further specified by economists. Its content could be spelled out as an optimal combination of economic sectors and subsectors ensuring maximum economic efficiency. For example, Georgia's GDP growth is mainly a result of the rapid growth of the financial sector and nor industry and this combination is responsible for the GDP's growth (around 12% in recent years). In our opinion this is not the optimal incentive for economic developments.

That is why the definition of "structural effect" is closely connected with the concept of a given state's comparative advantage. 5)

How can the "structural effect" be measured? There is no simple answer to this question. Evidently, it is a matter of definiteness, the share of key (core) sectors in the total effect, with possible changes in the content of the structural effect in view of progress. The general point is the optimal use of comparative advantages through global trade.

One-off injections into a country's economy (say, in the form of foreign investment) cannot reflect the "structural effect," although they can produce changes over the long term.

5) A sufficiently complete analysis of the comparative advantages of the countries of the Central Caucasus is given in the following articles: V. Papava, "Comparative Advantages of the Central Caucasian Countries: Potential, Realized, and Missed Opportunities, The Caucasus & Globalization, Vol. 1 (1), 2006, pp. 87-96; S. Zhukov, O. Reznikova, "Eco nomic Interaction in the Post-Soviet Space," The Caucasus & Globalization, Vol. 1 (1), 2006, pp. 96-109.

Globalization: A Challenge to National Economic Models?

Globalization 6) in the broad sense of the word implies the interdependence of states and nations in the performance of the socioeconomic function. A distinction should be drawn between the political, economic, technological and cultural components of globalization. Although there are no clear dividing lines between them (for example, economic decisions taken at the supranational level often have a negative political effect and vice versa), let us take a brief look at their content.

The second problem arising in this context is how to measure globalization, especially its economic component. In our opinion, there should be different approaches to various aspects of globalization depending on the content of the phenomenon, i.e., qualitative definiteness is the key to quantitative definiteness.

- The political component of globalization implies the interdependence of states based on common political interests (for example, the creation of the European Union), establishment of regional associations as a means of resolving political problems, etc.
- The economic component is based on a community of economic interests (trade and provision of services) aimed at maximizing the economic effect.
- The technological component implies technical progress (primarily in transport and communications) and contributes to the interdependence of countries. Moreover, the very process of globalization initiates an active search in the field of information and communication technologies.
- The cultural component is based on the multilevel development of cultures, religions and traditions.
- The political component of globalization in the Central Caucasus varies from country to country. On the one hand, Azerbaijan and Georgia are oriented toward Western values, and on the other, Armenia takes a pro-Russian stand. Such a choice makes some concrete alterations to the political actions of the region's countries; it is also bound to have an effect on their economic decisions. Another important aspect of this problem is the question of territorial integrity of Azerbaijan and Georgia 7).

6) The Globalization problem is investigated in many books and articles (see, for example: The Globalization of World Politics. An Introduction to International Relations, Second Edition, ed. by John Baylis and Steve Smith, Oxford University Press, Oxford, 2001; "Tired of Globalization, The Economist, November 2005; D. Held, "Democracy, the Nation-State and the Global System," Economy and Society, Vol. 20 (2), 1991, pp. 138-172; P. Krugman, "Growing World Trade: Causes and Consequences." Brookings Papers on Economic Activity, No. 1, 1995, pp. 327-377.

A natural question arising in this context is whether globalization (its political aspect) helps to resolve the problems of territorial integrity. The answer lies in the effectiveness of the activity of international institutions and organizations, and also in the appropriateness of actions taken by the parties concerned.

The basis for the solution of this problem is the following: the concept of "national," as pointed out above, should be inherent to state entities, in contrast to "national" as an inherent attribute of a certain ethnos. In the latter case, one can only speak of national sovereignty where the actor is a nation (ethnos). A confusion of the concepts of state and national sovereignties or their identification is unwarranted. This is evident, for example, from the fact that some national state and territorial entities proclaim their sovereignty, confusing national sovereignty and state sovereignty, which can and must be inherent only to the state. Another concept used in this context is "popular sovereignty" (sovereignty of the people), where the people are the key actor. The legal nature of the sovereign rights of the above-listed actors differs. In civil society, it is the population-as the citizens of a given state that constitutes a nation. That is why the concept of "national statehood," in contrast to social, has a general civil meaning in international practice, i.e., in this context the concepts of "nation" and "state" appear as synonyms.

It should also be noted that in cases where the emergence of nations on the whole happened at the same time as did the formation of centralized states, nations naturally took a state form and developed into independent nation-states (England, France, Italy). In the east of Europe, on the other hand, the formation of centralized states, accelerated by the need for self-defense (against invasions by the Turks, Mongols, etc.), preceded the emergence of nations. That is why in such cases the latter did not and could not develop into nation states, but formed several multinational states (Austria, Hungary, Russia).

The economic component of globalization should be analyzed with due regard for global contradictions:

Western integration contrasts with Eastern disintegration (to a certain extent). Supranational political integration in the West is accompanied by disintegration of states in the East;

7) According to experts, Georgia annually loses 20-30% of its GDP due to its territorial integrity problem (to some extent this also applies to Azerbaijan),

Economics and politics are increasingly internationalized in the sense of a common understanding of problems and decision making. At the same time, the importance of regional associations tends to increase;

European integration, nation states and regional associations-all these realities will continue to influence the political orientation of Europeans.

Above, we mentioned the indicators of globalization. On the economic side, one can speak about trade and its influence on the dynamics of the gross domestic product; about the dynamics of foreign investment (including direct investment); about the creation of multinational companies, etc.

If we look at the GDP, for example, we will find that in 2005, compared to the previous year, it increased by 26.4% in Azerbaijan, by 9.3% in Georgia, and by 14% in Armenia (in the past ten years, the overall GDP growth in the countries of the Central Caucasus averaged about 5%). it should also be mentioned that whereas, due to the 1998 global financial crisis, Georgia's GDP increased by 3.1% in 1998 and 2.9% in 1999, the respective figures for Azerbaijan were 10.0% and 7.4%, and for Armenia 7.3% and 3.3%.

As regards commerce, we are naturally dealing here, in the first place, with foreign trade (exports and imports). According to WTO data, a higher level of foreign trade operations means more effective economic development, faster GDP growth and lower transaction costs.

It is also difficult to overestimate the role of foreign investment, such as investment in the construction of the Baku-Tbilisi-Ceyhan (BTC) oil pipeline, which largely accounts for GDP growth in Georgia and Azerbaijan.

Plans of a global nature can only be implemented through the establishment of companies: multinational corporations (MNCs) and transnational Baku – Tbilisi - Ceyhan (BTC) and Transport Corridor Europe Caucasus Asia (TRACECA) projects.

The difficulties in Georgian- Russian relationships are mainly related with the "frozen" conflicts in breakaway regions of Abkhazia and South Ossetia. These tensions reached the culmination in the five days War in August, 2008. Georgia accuses Russia of imperialism, while Russia criticises Georgia for nationalism and pursuing an anti-Russian foreign policy. However the conflict has an economic dimension too. Many observers consider the economic policy of Russian Federation towords the former Soviet Republics Including Georgia as an agressive, so called "liberal empire" tool to restore its influence. The active participation of the russian enterprises in georgian privatization and investment processes (energy sector), opening of their subsidiaries in industry and banking sectors (Vneshtorgbank) are seen as the economic measures interrelated with political interests.

Finally, we can say with certainty that globalization has an institutional component as
well. It is the functioning of international economic organizations and institutions (like the World Bank, the International Monetary Fund (IMF) or the European Bank for Reconstruction and Development (EBRD). They have made and continue to make a tangible contribution to the development of the Central Caucasian countries, especially at the early stages of the transition period.

The technological component 8) of globalization is largely the result of scientific and technological progress, while technological determinism is the main driving force behind social development. New technologies are the key element in the globalization of culture, transport and communications, they reduce so-called transaction costs, thus promoting the growth of the economy and enhancing its efficiency.

The cultural component is quite important today, because it implies the need to take into account the multivariant and multi-vector nature of the world community (otherwise it would be featureless and uninteresting). There are many examples in today's world in which cultural circumstances and the factor of tradition have a significant positive effect 9 on economic progress 9).

States lacking self-sufficiency are more dependent on globalization and have more to gain from it.

Does globalization lead to general well-being or, on the contrary, intensify the struggle for survival? There appears to be no simple answer to this question, but it is a fact that the world has become "smaller" and that countries and organizations are more dependent on their "neighbors," competitors and partners than before.

Regional Economic Integration as a Way to Join the World Economy

It is no accident that the problems of the regional economy and regional economic integration have come on the agenda. This is dictated by the inner logic of economic research: the region is a major element in the self-organization of economic life. Soviet regional studies developed as a science dealing with the location of production and creation of territorial complexes. Later on, it began to study such areas of the regional economy as housing construction, urban development

8) See, for example: Daniele Archibugi, Jonathan Michie, "The Globalization of Technology: A New Taxonomy," in: Technology, Globalization and Economic Performance/ ed. by Daniele Archibugi and J. Michie, Cambridge University Press, Cambridge, 1997.

9) See, for example: M. Porter, H. Takeuchi, M. Sakakibara, Can Japan Compete? Basic Books and Perseus Publishing, New York, 2000.

communal property, real estate and land management. in Western economic literature, the region (in the economic sense of the word) is seen as a territorial unit that "resolves" certain socioeconomic problems.

Our analysis is concerned with regional economic integration of independent states as subjects of political power. In this case, the territory of the Central Caucasus is regarded as a single region 10). Within the framework of a general methodological analysis of this question, we leave aside the region's taxonomic rank, although it is obvious that each rank of this kind has its own specific features.

In our opinion, the effect of regional economic integration can be achieved in two ways: by integration within the region (Central Caucasus) and then (time of integration. depends on two factors: political stability in the region, economic speed of economic reforms) integration into the world community. This is the optimal alternative and effective, primarily from an economic standpoint.

As regards the first way, let us emphasize that, in principle, economic cooperation between the countries of the Central Caucasus is possible and necessary. In fact, this is how things stand in practice, although for well-known non-economic reasons the potential for such cooperation remains partly "untapped."

The second way is clear enough: the three republics should take part in global economic relations, but the question here is whether this is more effectively achieved through regional integration or through multi-speed and multi-vector steps. The answer here is obvious: the first option is more effective in view of economic factors.

Here we can refer to such concepts as "comparative advantage" and "structural effect." The 'structural effect" is more peculiar for "small" and "transitional countries, because of the non-stability of the economy and the short-term change in demand. Due to these circumstances, the involvement of the Central Caucasian countries in the global economy through regional economic integration will be much more effective, because the realization of their economic potentials in this case will mean lower costs and, accordingly, will have a more significant effect.

10) The basic methodological premises of this approach are given in E. Ismailov's article, "New Regionalism in the Caucasus: A Conceptual Approach" (see: E. Ismailov, op. cit.). Based on historical analysis, the author rightly believes that the historical process "shows the... trends toward regional integration. In other words, the Caucasus is bound to form a single and integral entity of globalization." (ibid., p. 13).

Conclusion

The question formulated in this article: "The National Economic Model alternative to Globalization?" is by no means a rhetorical one. The answer to it, in our opinion, is as follows: this model will be an alternative if national economic interests and the comparative advantages of states in the interdependent world are not taken into account. At the same time, it will not be an alternative if the globalization process equally ensures economic growth in our interrelated, globalized world. This means, as we see it, that economic globalization will help each country to realize its comparative advantages, while regional economic integration-as a factor of gradual entry into the global economy-will come into full play.

Globalization should provide opportunities for using the economic potentials (in other words, the comparative advantages) of the Central Caucasian states. The existence of certain noneconomic problems (political problems in the first place) is further evidence of the truth about the interconnection between economics and politics.

Investment Capacity of the Country's Economy (The Case of Georgia)

Abstract
The article discusses the factors of the functioning of the economy - land, capital, labour. Particular attention is paid to the issues of investment in these factors and their capacity. The idea of measuring the investment intensity of the country's economy is proposed – in qualitative and quantitative terms. In the first case, we are talking about the content of investments in industry, agriculture, construction, financial services, non-manufacturing, etc., in the second case, about the volume of these investments. The hypothesis is put forward that excessive investment in the country's economy can cause the economy to overheat, as well as contribute to the emergence of corruption in society and the economy, which slows down its economic growth. The so-called "production possibilities curve" can conditionally act as a limiter of excessive investments in the economy. The upper point located outside the curve of production capabilities (inaccessibility) can be conditionally considered a point indicating the inexpediency of excessive investment.

Keywords: *Investment; factors of the functioning of the economy; investment capacity; curve of production capabilities; overheating of the economy; corruption; investment policy.*

Qualitative Determinants of Investments

Investment (German Investition, from Latin investio - I dress), a long-term investment of capital in industry, agriculture, transport, services and other sectors of the economy both within the country and abroad in order to make a profit.

In the economic literature, financial and real investments differ. Financial investment - investments in stocks, bonds and other securities issued by corporations or the state*. Real investment – investment of capital in the creation of new capital goods, involves the formation of new capital (capital formation) or net capital additions to existing capital goods. Investments include investments in fixed production capital (buildings, structures, equipment) housing, construction, inventory (raw materials, materials, finished products and production in progress). Gross investments, net of depreciation amounts of fixed capital, represent net investments. From the point of view of the sectoral approach to investments in the economy, state financial participation is necessary (for example, a partner fund in Georgia), the financial policy of the state should be manifested in this.

Hence, investment is the process of adding to stocks of real productive assets. This may mean acquiring fixed assets, such as building, plant, or equipment, or adding to stocks and work in progress. This is the Keynesian definition of investment: it is a flow concept. Investment goods are goods designed to be used for investment rather than consumption (1).

Once again about the factor analysis of the functioning of the economy

It is well known that factor analysis is a multidimensional method for studying the relationships between the values of variables. At the same time, these relationships can manifest themselves at different levels of the economy both in vertical (enterprise, sub-sectors, industries) and spatial aspects (regional economies). In our article, we focus on the macro-approach ("large line of development"), that is, on the factors that determine the functioning of the economy as a whole within one country. And in this context, the investment process plays a special role in the factors of the functioning and growth of the economy.

In the beginning (according to the classical approach, the factors of production meant land, capital, labor force, but as economic theory and practice developed, the factors of entrepreneurship (Joseph Schumpeter, who called entrepreneurship a special economic factor in addition to the three well-known ones – land, capital, labor) and the state were involved. Regarding the latter factor, the position of a scientist-economist, academician of the Academy of Sciences of Georgia, Vladimir Papava, is quite interesting, when the functioning of the state is possible at the expense of private borrowing, and not on the basis of receiving taxes (2).

In the economic literature, when there is a talk about factors of production, we are talking about their efficiency (return), to a lesser extent about their capacity. So, for example, when it comes to land (land resources), they use indicators of the area of land resources, how effectively this resource is used, what is the yield per hectare (in the case of agriculture), etc. In the case of capital, it is capital return. In the case of labor there is used productivity for each unit of output. It is relatively difficult to measure entrepreneurship, entrepreneurial ability (although indirectly it can be determined indirectly, for example, by the profit indicator). And as for the state, here you can use indicators of fulfilling your obligations to the population of the country: financial, social, etc. As for the capacity of these factors, quantification is much more complicated here and depends on the needs of the development of the economy and society, and these needs vary over time.

The issue of sources of investment (opportunities) is also relevant: the main sources of investment are profit and savings (as part of disposable income). The latter factor is thoroughly disclosed in the main work of John Maynard Keynes (3), while Keynes considers savings as the basis of demand, recovery of the economy from the crisis and further growth.

On the role of investments and investment capacity in the economy

Investment refers to those economic (financial) resources that are directed to increase the real capital of the company, for example, to expand or modernize the production apparatus. This may be due to the purchase of new cars, buildings, vehicles, as well as the construction of roads, bridges and other engineering structures. It is necessary to include here the costs of education and scientific research. These costs represent a cumulative investment in human capital and also increase the productive potential of the economy.

An investment is essentially an asset that is created with the intention of allowing money to grow. One, if you invest in a saleable asset, you may earn income by way of profit. Second, if investments are made in a return generating plan, then you will earn an income via accumulation of gain. There are a few types of investments: Growth, Shares, Property, Defensive investments, Cash, Fixed interest.

Excessive investment slows down the growth of the economy corruption, which can cause such phenomena as the shadow economy, underutilization of production capacity, overheating of the economy, loss of public confidence, social disasters, etc.

Usually, statistical-economists, when quantifying investment opportunities, use the ratio of investment volume to gross domestic product I/GDP (t), and everything is logical here, since GDP is a comprehensive indicator of economic performance (despite some of its weaknesses, for example, not taking into account the quality of life, the shadow and informal economy). It seems to us that here it is necessary to supplement the above-mentioned indicator from the structural approach. In general, the use of the method of structural levels (as an epistemological tool of cognition) in the analysis of economics enriches the tools of economic science.

We offer a formula for calculating the investment intensity of a country by vector calculation of the investment intensity of the country's economy (both developed and medium-developed, developing and transitional):

I (investment intensity) (t) = X (I/Land(t) + I/Capital(t) + I/Labor) (t), where I is the volume of internal and external investments, X is a certain country; L is the territory of land resources; C is capital; L is labor; (t) is a period of time.

It should be taken into account that in the current century (2001-2020), foreign direct investment accounted for only 1/3 (33.1%) of the total cost of investment in the national economy of Georgia, and the share of "local variety" investment - more than 2/3 (66.9%). The total value of the enlarged components of the national wealth of Georgia (land, taking into account hydromineral resources and forests, national property and human capital – excluding financial capital) in the middle of the second decade of the twenty–first century amounted to approximately 410 billion US dollars, including land - 90 billion US dollars; elements of national property – $200 billion, and human capital – $120 billion. With this in mind, the investment capacity of the land was 4.0%, the national property - 10.0%, and the labor force (human capital) - 18.8%. In general, the investment capacity of the country was:

I (investment capacity) (2001-2020) = 0.22*4.0% + 0.488*10.0% + 0.292*18.8% = 11.3%

Statistical-economists usually calculate such an important indicator as the I/GDP ratio, but it shows the scale of investments in the economy as a whole (which is very important from the point of view of macroeconomics) and not factorially. Over the first two decades of the twentieth century (2001-2020), the investment capacity of Georgia's GDP averaged 8.9%. At the same time, it had its maximum value in 2007 (17.3%); in 2001, its level did not exceed 3.4%, and in 2020, due to the pandemic and the decline in business activity on a global scale, it accounted for only 3.9% - almost 2 times less than in the previous year (2019 3.9%). **

The question naturally arises: what should be the optimal investment capacity of the countries? The answer to this question is quite difficult, and that's why: firstly, the uniformity and diversity of economic processes; secondly, the content and direction of the financial and economic policy of the state; thirdly, the market environment in the world economy.

Here we are conditionally considering the problem with the phenomenon of production capabilities (and the corresponding curve) and that's why: the upper point is beyond the reach of the economy. It can be achieved in conditions of investment growth (both internal and external), but this can lead to both overheating of the economy and corruption phenomena). And here the question arises: to what extent is the capacity of the economy (its functioning factors) adequate to this process?

The indicator of investment intensity can be used in the analysis of issues of economic growth of a country, although it does not have absolute significance, since other important factors have a significant impact on economic growth, ranging from the level of political stability in the country to market conditions (both internal and external). Indicative in this respect is the volatility of the correlation between the investment intensity calculated in relation to foreign direct investment to GDP and the growth rate of GDP itself. So, for the period from 2001 to 2020, it (the difference between these indicators) ranged from - 3.0% in 2003 to 10.1% in 2020.

On the basis of which investment decisions are made. Based on intuition? The psychological factor in the economy? Irrational behavior? (4) I think that partially, yes. After all, investing is the action of a subjective factor in the economy (government, companies, households [through savings]).

It should be noted that both in the Soviet economic literature and in practice, indicators were used – capital intensity, capital return, capital intensity and capital return (5). But two circumstances should be noted: a) the Soviet model of the economy implied a single country, the so-called unified national economic complex (UNEC), when the formation of fixed assets (capital) on the basis of centralized planning; b) the ownership of the funds was state (nationwide) I do not touch here on the question of the forms of manifestation of this property, because this is a big topic and goes beyond the scope of this article, especially since very often both economists and lawyers confuse the economic and legal aspects of property. Meanwhile, the truth, as always, is in the middle: legal - what belongs to whom, economic - what is the material result.

About the overheating of the economy

When the economy overheats some producers are not able to supply all the goods that consumers demand. This can lead to prices rising faster than they otherwise would. Overheating can also make household and firms over-optimistic about their future income prospects, and lead them to take on too much debt. Overheating of the economy is a real threat to countries with unstable economies, developing (transition) economies, as well as highly specialized regions, when GDP growth is 8-12 percent for 2-3 consecutive years. The danger is that if the growth rates are very high, for one reason or another that is not related to production, a situation may turn out when macroeconomic indicators deteriorate (for example, inflation). A difficult situation may arise for Georgia, when high economic growth is necessary to overcome the lag of previous years, on the other hand, growth may contribute to overheating of the economy.

Overheating of the economy is a situation in which the pace of economic growth becomes explosive uncontrollable and, having absorbed all the resources of the private and public sector, they come close to the line beyond which further sustainable growth exhausts itself and a recession begins. The overheating of the economy is preceded by excessive financing of growth, over-crediting, excessive investment of public funds in the economy, the state budget deficit is taking on threatening proportions, inflation, the value of the foreign trade balance is increasingly going into negative territory or sharply decreasing. Economic agents anticipating the approach of a recession prefer to invest in the real sector of the economy - for example, real estate, rather than financial instruments (bonds, stocks, etc.). Among the symptoms of overheating of the economy, many economists, financiers emphasize overinvestment in economic funds (goods and equipment, services, capital caused by the low price of borrowed money (Central Bank interest rates), or high consumer demand, or international market conditions (price conditions), or speculative boom caused by new investment opportunities in the economy as a whole or in individual industries. Overheating of the economy can be accompanied by both inflation and deflation (due to an increase in the supply of material goods and services). Usually it (overheating) is accompanied by high (well above average) economic growth rates, growth of commodity and stock markets, moderate or low price of credit money. In other words, the overheating of the economy is caused by the excessive influence of the state through the Central Bank on the credit market. Under these conditions, the planning of monetary policy by the state in market conditions cannot reflect the needs and trends of economic development, which leads to overinvestment of capital by entrepreneurs who focus on the bank interest rate and overconsumption by individuals who also focus on interest rates. And, finally, overheating of the economy is fraught with economic recession, unemployment, and a drop in the standard of living of the population. And the latter reduces the saved part of household income, which in itself is a source of investment in the economy.

Overheating of the economy can also contribute to an excessive amount of investment with all the negative consequences that follow from this, as mentioned above. Naturally, it contributes to the overheating of the economy with all the negative consequences that follow from this. Therefore, the investment policy of the state should be aimed at balancing the growth of the economy and the volume of investments.

On corruption in economy

Corruption "The use of bribery to influence politicians, civil servants, and other officials" (6). Economics of corruption deals with misuse of public for private benefit and its economic impact on society. Economies that are afflicted by a high level of corruption are not capable of prospering as fully as those with a low of corruption. Also, economies that are corrupted are not able to function properly since the natural laws of the economy can not function freely. As a consequence, corruption for instance, leads to *inefficient allocation of resources,* poor education, and healthcare or the presence of shadow economy that includes illegal activities as well as unreported income from production legal goods and services for which taxes should be paid, but are not (7,8).

Investors often seek a fair competitive, business environment, thus they will mostly avoid investing in countries where there is a high level of corruption. Studies show a positive relationship between the level of corruption in a country and measurements of the competitiveness of its environment (9).

Corruption breeds inefficiencies that may affect the static level of output. In order for corruption to affect economic growth, capital accumulation, or total factor productivity. As 1995 study by Paulo Mauro (10) shows that capital accumulation, in the *form of investment,* is negatively correlated with corruption, particularly *foreign direct investment* (11).

Corruption is a global phenomenon that causes poverty, obstructs development and drives away *investment.* It also debilitates the judicial and political systems that should be working for the public good. Not surprisingly, as the rule of law is weakened and the voice of the people remains unheard, citizens trust in government officials and national institutions dwindles.

The problem of corruption in society is multi-layered, multi-level (sectoral and territorial levels). In our article we give an analysis of corruption that has arisen in the economy (including non-payment of taxes) (12), in particular, corruption resulting from the influx of a large volume (capacity) of investments. But there are other levels of corruption – in various organizations (for example, in the banking sector), etc.

According to the level of corruption (its perception), Georgia ranks 45th among 145 countries. The word perception refers to the subjective opinion of the interviewed subjects (this is very conditional). At the same time, of course, the articles of the Criminal Code of Georgia clearly define the level of punishment for specific facts of this phenomenon, and of course everything is decided by the court.

About the investment policy of the government

It is well known that the economic policy of the government means the actions of the government to implement the requirements of objective economic laws. At the same time, there may be some difference between the essence and the form of manifestation of these laws. Economic policy is also a question of priorities and choices, bearing in mind that economic problems require solutions that contradict each other (for example, investments from the investor's point of view, this is one thing, and from the government's point of view, this is another. And in this context, investment policy as an organic part of investment policy acquires a special role.

Investment policy, according to American Professor William Sharp (Nobel Laureate,1990), is an integral part of the investment process, including the definition of an investor's goals, his preferences between expected return and risk (13). Elements of investment policy: the types of assets in which the investor invests; the degree of activity of investment portfolio management; the choice as the purpose of investment - income generation or asset value growth (Ibid).

The investment policy of the state (macro level) is a set of interrelated goals and measures to ensure the necessary level and structure of investments in the country's economy and its individual spheres and industries, increasing the investment activity of all the main agents of the economy: the population, entrepreneurs, etc. In other words, investments from the point of view of the country as a whole are investments in the creation of new or replacement of worn–out industrial, human or natural capital. The investment policy of the state should be aimed at attracting investments in innovative industries in the economy and beyond (science, biotechnology, architecture, computers, automotive, interaction with the outside world, ecology, medicine, robotics).

The investment policy of the enterprise (micro-level) is a part of the economic and financial strategy of the enterprise. It consists in choosing and implementing the most effective forms of its real and financial investments in order to ensure high rates of its development and a constant increase in its market value. Investments should contribute to the production of competitive products in order to gain their own niche both in the foreign market and in the domestic market, and for this it is necessary to meet at least three conditions: a) the volume of products; b) the quality of products; c) the price per unit of production. Product volume growth can be achieved with the inclusion of additional investments in (fixed capital, investments, human capital); improvement of product quality depends on competition in the market (rejection of protectionist policies); pricing, in turn, depends on the first two factors – the larger the volume of output, the lower the cost of each subsequent output (scale effect) and, accordingly, the price, which determines profit (at the micro level). As for the macro aspect, it ultimately affects the efficiency of the country's economy as a whole.

As known, the fundamental uncertainty of the market (which causes market failures) determines the need to strengthen the regulatory function of the government using various tools (primarily tax policy). Regarding the economic policy that should be carried out for the purpose of optimal investment policy, we can talk about a certain **divestition - the opposite of investment**. Divestition (Eng. divestment, divestiture) withdrawal of capital investments, sale of part of assets or the entire company. With divestition, proceeds from the sale of assets usually exceed future cash flows from their further operation (a well-known example is the Finnish *Nokia* group, which sold off non-telecommunications divisions in the early 90s. This is usually used at the level of firms, companies, that is, at the level of microeconomics, but I think that this tool can be used at the level of macroeconomics, that is, within the whole country. How? With the same tax policy pursued by the state: providing the most favored-nation treatment to those investors who will invest in those industries in the development of which the state is interested. You can object to me: just a paragraph above, I called for the rejection of protectionist measures in order to improve product quality, but in this case we have a special circumstance - when the state is interested in attracting **optimal investments, not maximum**, and therefore an exception can be made here (recall the famous aphorism "there are no rules without exception" – every rule has its exception - a saying from the words of the Roman stoic philosopher Seneca).

Instead of conclusion

The idea of writing this short article appeared relatively recently due to the importance of increasing the maximum amount of investment, both on the part of the state and on the part of economic scientists (representatives of the mass media did not stand aside either). Meanwhile, we see the main problem in attracting not maximum, but optimal investments in relevant sectors of the economy for Georgia, taking into account an innovative approach. That is why the article suggests the ***investment capacity*** indicator, which, in our opinion, can be taken into account by the state when developing and conducting the country's investment policy.

The appendix to the article contains diagrams reflecting the dynamics of foreign direct investment (FDI) in the Georgian economy.

References

1. A Dictionary of Economics (1997) John Black. Oxford New York. Oxford University Press. P.251;

2. Папава Владимир. (1993) Государство рынок и экономика. Препринт. Академия Наук Грузии. Институт экономики им. П. Гугушвили. – 36 С.;

3. J. M.Keynes „The GENERAL THEORY of Employment Interest and Money".New York Harcout, Brace and Company, 1936; в русском переводе с.116-120;

4. Акерлофф Дж., Шиллер Р. (2010) Spiritus Animals. М., С.177;

5. Экономическая энциклопедия. Политическая экономия (1975) М., том 2. С.118-119; та же энциклопедия (1980) М., том 4. С. 314-316;

6. A Dictionary of Economics (1977) John Black. Oxford New York. Oxford University Press. P.93;

7, 8. How Corruption Affects Emerging Economies. In: Investopedia. 19.05.2019 [cit.2020-03-21]; Ibid.;

9. The Institutional Economics of Corruption and Reform: Theory, evidence, and policy. ISBN 978-0-521-87275-1;

10. The Quarterly Journal of Economics (1995) Volume 110, Issue 3, August, pp. 681-712, https://doi.org/10.2307/2946696;

11. Wei, Shang-Jin (2000) "How taxing is corruption on international investors?". Review of economics and statistics 82.1: pp.1-11;

12. Shevardnadze K., Chechelashvili R., Chocheli V., Khaduri N. (2000) PAPAVA INDEXEX OF TAX CORRUPTION. Publisher "Company Imperial" Ltd. Tbilisi. – pp.31-47;

13. Уильям Ф. Шарп, Гордон Дж. Александер, Джеффри В. Бейли (2016) Инвестиции. М.: Изд-во Инфра -М., С.780-789;

* In the article "state" and "government" we use as synonyms.

**Calculations were carried out by Iosif Archvadze, Professor of Kutaisi University.

Appendix

1.

FDI IN GEORGIA IN 2019-2021

(MILLION US DOLLARS)

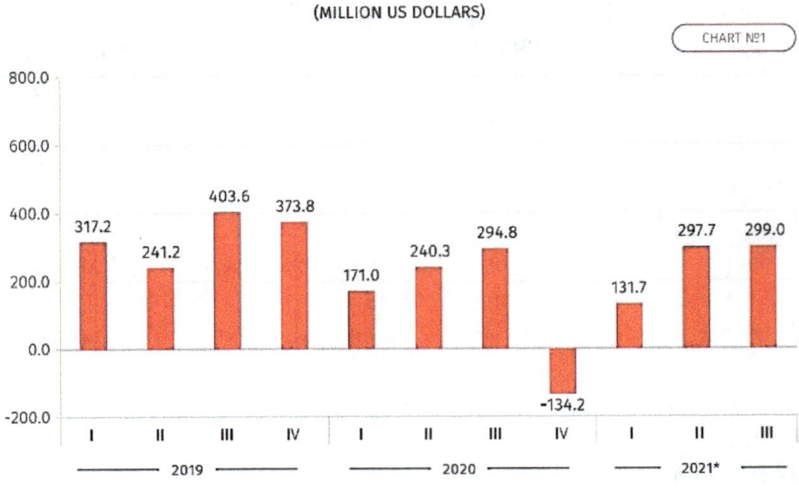

*Preliminary data.

Source: National Statistics Office of Georgia https://www.geostat.ge/en (last seen 9.12.2021)

TABLE №2

DYNAMICS OF FDI IN GEORGIA

(MILLION US DOLLARS)

YEAR	I	II	III	IV	TOTAL
2006	145.2	318.0	332.4	375.5	**1 171.2**
2007	330.8	375.3	470.6	588.0	**1 764.7**
2008	540.1	607.7	136.1	291.3	**1 575.2**
2009	114.5	178.3	179.1	194.9	**666.8**
2010	176.1	211.5	236.8	241.2	**865.6**
2011	222.6	273.1	309.1	329.2	**1 134.0**
2012	312.4	248.0	220.5	267.3	**1 048.2**
2013	291.8	224.1	271.6	251.6	**1 039.2**
2014	331.9	217.6	749.5	538.0	**1 837.0**
2015	343.4	493.2	531.1	361.0	**1 728.8**
2016	392.9	452.6	507.8	300.6	**1 654.0**
2017	413.3	396.6	635.4	535.4	**1 980.8**
2018	329.3	408.1	367.2	212.4	**1 317.1**
2019	317.2	241.2	403.6	373.8	**1 335.8**
2020	171.0	240.3	294.8	-134.2	**572.0**
2021*	131.7	297.7	299.0		**728.4**

Source: National Statistics Office of Georgia https://www.geostat.ge/en (last seen 9.12.2021)

3.

TABLE №3

FDI IN GEORGIA BY COMPONENTS IN 2019-2021

(MILLION US DOLLARS)

	2019				TOTAL	2020				TOTAL	2021*		
	I	II	III	IV		I	II	III	IV		I	II	III
TOTAL	**317.2**	**241.2**	**403.6**	**373.8**	**1 335.8**	**171.0**	**240.3**	**294.8**	**-134.2**	**572.0**	**131.7**	**297.7**	**299.0**
of which:													
Equity	109.6	154.0	268.7	171.6	**704.0**	42.1	130.3	93.1	-236.8	**28.7**	28.4	38.4	16.8
Reinvestment of earnings^	123.3	88.5	239.0	184.2	**635.1**	114.6	133.7	123.2	129.0	**500.5**	72.0	247.9	293.3
Debt instruments^^	84.2	-1.3	-104.1	17.9	**-3.2**	14.3	-23.7	78.5	-26.4	**42.8**	31.3	11.4	-11.0

*Preliminary data.

^ Reinvestment of earnings - difference between profit/loss and dividends.

^^ Debt instruments- includes trade credits and loans.

Source: National Statistics Office of Georgia https://www.geostat.ge/en (last seen 9.12.2021)

4.

TABLE №4

MAJOR INVESTOR COUNTRIES BY Q3 2021

(MILLION US DOLLARS)

	2019				TOTAL	2020				TOTAL	2021*		
	I	II	III	IV		I	II	III	IV		I	II	III
TOTAL	**317.2**	**241.2**	**403.6**	**373.8**	**1 335.8**	**171.0**	**240.3**	**294.8**	**-134.2**	**572.0**	**131.7**	**297.7**	**299.0**
of which:													
United Kingdom	56.8	-22.3	81.1	121.3	**236.9**	72.0	59.2	115.2	56.6	**303.0**	88.4	121.8	60.9
Netherlands	-81.8	65.9	49.6	54.4	**88.1**	21.7	68.8	90.5	19.6	**200.7**	5.6	41.0	59.8
Czech Republic	-11.7	13.6	13.0	2.6	**17.6**	-3.0	0.1	5.7	-9.8	**-7.0**	14.1	30.9	36.0
United States	21.4	27.3	40.7	26.2	**115.6**	30.7	22.6	26.2	18.9	**98.4**	-59.8	0.4	29.6
Turkey	69.0	51.1	-20.6	74.7	**174.2**	13.9	26.2	-3.6	42.6	**79.0**	28.9	22.4	24.2
Malta	-35.4	8.0	15.9	12.7	**1.2**	10.2	19.3	4.5	11.9	**45.9**	-11.9	8.8	15.8
France	2.0	3.7	5.6	8.8	**20.1**	0.2	1.8	1.4	8.4	**11.8**	1.0	3.0	14.5
Seychelles	0.3	0.5	1.6	0.7	**3.1**	0.7	-1.5	0.1	-0.2	**-0.9**	1.6	2.4	13.0
Russia	7.0	7.5	24.7	16.0	**55.2**	14.1	7.0	8.3	9.8	**39.2**	32.0	8.8	12.5
Other countries	289.6	86.0	192.0	56.3	**623.9**	10.4	36.9	46.6	-292.0	**-198.2**	31.8	58.1	32.8

Source: National Statistics Office of Georgia https://www.geostat.ge/en (last seen 9.12.2021)

5.

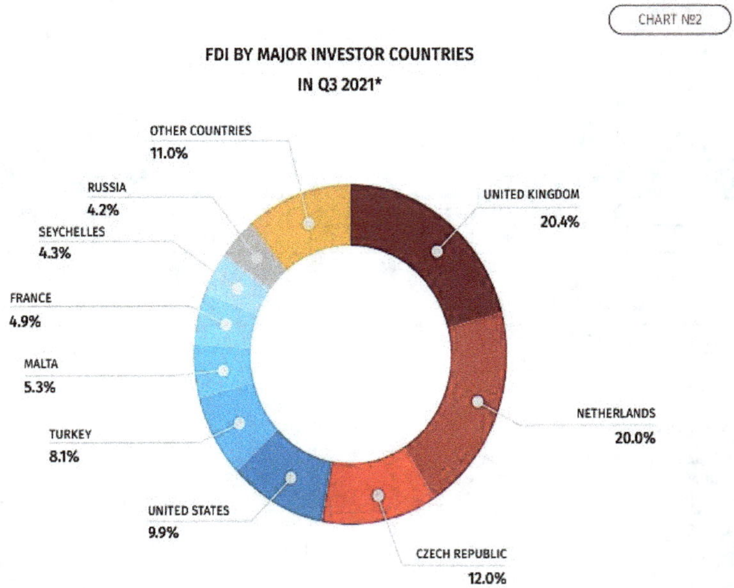

Source: National Statistics Office of Georgia https://www.geostat.ge/en (last seen 9.12.2021)

6.

TABLE №5

FDI BY ECONOMIC SECTORS IN 2019-2021

(MILLION US DOLLARS)

	2019				TOTAL	2020				TOTAL	2021*		
	I	II	III	IV		I	II	III	IV		I	II	III
TOTAL	**317.2**	**241.2**	**403.6**	**373.8**	**1 335.8**	**171.0**	**240.3**	**294.8**	**-134.2**	**572.0**	**131.7**	**297.7**	**299.0**
of which:													
Financial sector	48.1	-24.3	106.5	141.8	**272.1**	96.6	79.5	129.8	98.4	**404.4**	98.0	139.3	87.1
Energy sector	71.2	87.9	49.4	52.9	**261.4**	-23.4	31.4	34.4	-50.1	**-7.8**	40.8	65.5	69.3
Manufacturing	25.3	41.3	50.8	0.0	**117.3**	5.3	15.9	29.0	-14.6	**35.5**	26.3	50.2	54.8
Transports	27.9	17.6	14.7	-5.2	**55.0**	7.9	3.7	-4.8	6.1	**12.8**	-5.1	-18.2	27.9
Construction	4.9	7.8	-11.5	44.8	**46.0**	-0.5	22.9	-12.7	23.6	**33.3**	2.1	-3.0	16.5
Communications	16.2	4.8	17.3	33.7	**72.1**	13.2	11.2	15.4	10.1	**49.9**	-68.7	-5.0	14.5
Health and social work	2.0	7.7	1.8	7.2	**18.8**	6.3	-1.1	1.6	3.7	**10.6**	12.0	5.4	7.5
Hotels and restaurants	57.8	21.8	36.7	7.0	**123.4**	7.4	-6.1	1.5	-252.4	**-249.5**	-0.9	-1.5	6.9
Agriculture, fishing	1.5	1.2	1.2	2.3	**6.3**	-3.7	5.0	-1.3	-1.8	**-1.8**	0.8	2.2	2.3
Other sectors	62.3	75.3	136.6	89.3	**363.4**	62.0	77.9	101.9	42.9	**284.6**	26.3	62.8	12.1

Source: National Statistics Office of Georgia https://www.geostat.ge/en (last seen 9.12.2021)

7.

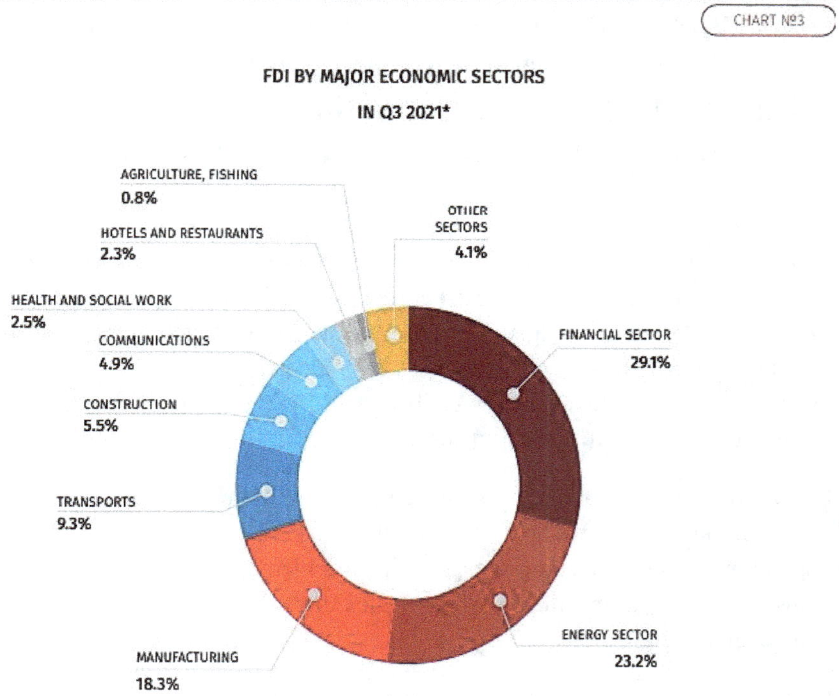

Source: National Statistics Office of Georgia https://www.geostat.ge/en (last seen 9.12. 2021

Occupational Analysis of Demand and Supply of Skilled Labor – a Cornerstone of Comprehensive Labor Market Information for TVET (Technical Vocational Education and Training) planning

Abstract

TVET and tertiary education systems are constantly under pressure to deliver graduates meeting the labor market demand. The performance of these systems is commonly judged by the: a) scale of shortages of skilled labor reported by employers, and b) surpluses of graduates, some of whom may be unemployed or employed in low-skilled or different occupations leading to occupational and qualification mismatches.

For various reasons, imbalances between the supply and demand for skilled labor may arise. For example, because the increasing education level of the population is outperforming the growth of skilled jobs in the economy, or industries do not absorb the TVET graduates. Also, trained persons may move abroad, etc.

Likewise, an imbalance in the occupational structure of the labor market could arise because TVET and the tertiary systems may continue delivering graduates in occupations that give them little or no chance of finding a job, as the local labor market may already be saturated with jobseekers with similar occupational profiles.
Key words: technical and vocational education and training; labor force; labor force market; qualification; information systems; demand and supply on labor force; labor force.

Introduction

Because of the lack of comprehensive labor market information (LMI) on shortages and surpluses of skilled labor or experience in its use, the TVET deliver training programs are usually (i) "student demand-driven" or (ii) determined by the availability of resources, instructors, and equipment.

In particular, the availability of LMI and its use in professional education programming help reduce risks of shortages and surpluses of skilled labor in the regional markets.

Most countries conduct a Labor Force Survey (LFS) collecting quarterly data on employment, unemployment and other population characteristics. Notably, an LFS collects data on the labor force occupational structure. The ISCO-08 Levels 3 and 4 (Minor and Unit groups) are the levels of detail required for a comprehensive analysis of labor force by individual occupations. Importantly, these levels should be used as LMI-based guidance for planning TVET delivery.

From the point of view of the analysis of the regional demand for skilled labor, the key task of professional education is to reproduce the employed skilled labor force (workforce) in line with the occupational job structure of the regional economy and its anticipated dynamics. The occupational and qualification structures of the workforce in a region are a proper foundation of the regional demand for TVET and tertiary graduates, which sets out the main direction of labor market analysis for advising TVET delivery planning.

Labor Market Information and Labor Market Information System

Labor market information is any information that assists people from various walks of life in making informed decisions about the labor market. LMI on occupations or industry, for example, can help you make essential decisions about study and training, your first job, or the next step in your career. Having quality and timely LMI also allows its users to prepare for the economy of tomorrow, by ensuring the right people are available for future work and also by encouraging the development of new skills which can take our economy in new, productive directions.

The best LMI provides users with information to make positive labor market changes that benefit everybody.

Labor market information system (LMIS) involves institutional arrangements, technology systems and procedures for collecting, processing, storing, retrieving, and disseminating labor market information. An LMIS provides an essential basis for employment and labor policies and informs the design, implementation, monitoring and evaluation of better-focused and targeted policies.

Most economically advanced countries have expanded the traditional mandate to analyze the current and anticipated demand for workforce and produce the employment scenarios for 10- 15 years by ISCO-08 (or its national equivalent) Major and Sub-major groups and industries at the national and regional levels. Hence, for the analysis of the demand and supply of skilled labor the key requirement to the LMIS is the production and access to the:

- Occupational analysis of the labor force at the ISCO-08 Level 4 (or its national equivalent); and
- Analysis of the unemployed by occupation in the previous job and by the field of study

In certain countries, LMIS is expected to steer the results of interaction between the demand and supply by capturing occupational and qualification mismatches in the labor markets. Since the operational focus is on regional labor markets, LMIS should have a precise regional dimension to guide the regional skills development systems.
LMIS should provide structured signals to the labor market authorities, agencies in charge of labor market guidance, professional education systems, and job seekers. These signals should be different to reflect the mandates and needs of multiple users.

Occupational analysis of demand and supply of skilled labor

The occupational structure of the workforce across regional industries reflects requirements for skilled labor by the number and structure of individual occupations. Only the professional education and training systems can produce specific number of professionals, technicians, and high-skilled workers and replenish the skilled workforce, if and when required.

Companies can provide only a limited number of skilled workers with on-the-job training, mainly in narrow operational competencies. Because companies do not deliver theoretical training, technicians and professionals cannot be trained on the job. Industries need a consistent supply of qualified labor in line with their occupational and qualification structures and labor turnover needs.

In periods of economic stability, occupational structures of industry workforces are not changing rapidly. The workforce occupational data produced from year to year become a basis for advising TVET delivery planning.

Analysis of demand for skilled labor should focus on the labor force's regional occupational and qualification structure, its growth/decline trends, and labor force turnover (separation from labor and change of occupation). These factors determine the overall need for producing TVET graduates.

Occupational vacancies generated by industries may be routinely filled by job seekers available in a region's labor market, leading to «zero jobs» in certain occupations available for fresh TVET graduates. If a regional TVET system plans its delivery based on the demand side estimates only, the risks of oversupply of certain occupations will increase. Some countries, such as the USA, produce regional/local forecasts of demand and estimates of future wages for occupations published in the Occupational Outlook Handbook. However, these forecasts are intended to serve as a labor market guidance for individuals and cannot serve as a solid basis for providing accurate advice for professional education systems.

If many individuals in the same location choose a career in the same occupation with high wages, then graduates in this occupation risk being oversupplied. A shortage in this occupation may occur if most individuals do not choose a particular occupational career.

For example, directors of Technical and Future Education (TAFE) colleges in Australia, managers of community colleges in the USA, directors of vocational colleges in France, etc., are required to produce evidence that they know the annual supply of graduates by training providers in their outreach areas. Each college in Australia is required to regularly produce a document called an «Environmental scan» containing estimates of the demand and supply by occupation. The additional demand for skilled labor should be measured using:
A National Classification of Occupation referring to job titles having standard occupational
names and codes corresponding to the TVET graduates' occupations.

should include data on:

a) Expected growth or decline of employment in each skilled occupation; and

b) Expected shortages or surpluses of skilled labor in each occupation to reflect the trend of increase or decrease caused by the industries' employment growth or decline.

Components of the additional demand for skilled labor

«Additional» demand includes the labor force necessary to satisfy:

- «Expansion demand» - growth/expansion of the industry employment, no matter the reason
- «Replacement demand») - replacing workers separating from jobs due to retirement, change of occupation, exiting the labor force, etc.

Both streams of demand exist in any economy. Notably, even if there is no employment expansion, the replacement demand exists almost always because of the regular labor turnover.

Reduction of employment may also happen when no additional jobs are forthcoming or when productivity growth reduces the need for more labor (meaning «no expansion demand»)

The demand-driven TVET delivery is based on understanding and responding to the additional demand for skilled labor. It is a way of reducing the risk of graduates becoming unemployed or mismatched at their jobs.

Trends of the additional demand across industries are commonly different for each occupation. Knowledge of the current skilled employment by occupation and the qualification level is the only basis for estimating the additional demand. The additional demand needs to be formulated using occupational titles and codes of the National Occupational Classification.

"Expansion" demand

The "expansion demand" for skilled labor is caused by creating new jobs due to various factors. Even a plain demographic growth inevitably results in the expansion of labor force – the employed and self- employed.

Companies belonging to the same industry have similarities in terms of products and technologies. They may also have similarities in the occupational structures of their workforces. Analysis of the expansion demand for skilled labor begins with the analysis of occupational structure in each regional industry. Some industries may gradually increase their employment, while others may experience a decline. A usual trend in many economies has been that agriculture (and manufacturing) shed labor, while employment in services increases.

Growth or decline of employment in specific industries may appear as a trend that continues for some years and allows for anticipating future short-term employment changes.

The "expansion demand" may result from requirements for more workers or fewer workers or workers in different occupations who should be hired due to the ongoing change in technologies and products. Regular analysis of the occupational structure of the labor force and production of the data series is the only way to document and forecast the occupational changes taking place. It is not uncommon, however, that the matching employment growth does not accompany the output growth in some industries because of the of setting effects of productivity growth.

«Replacement demand» for skilled labor

The "replacement demand" arises as a need to replace employees who are separated from jobs due to death, sickness, maternity leave, migration, or exiting the labor force or occupation. The need to replace employees varies considerably across industries, occupations and between seasons.

In producing long-term employment forecasts, the probability of employees quitting their jobs due to retirement, death and accidents may be modelled by using the method of age group shifts and calculation of labor shares reaching the retirement age. Accident rates are also calculated, varying by country, industry, etc.

An occupational labor turnover is another cause of replacement demand. When skilled workers move between companies without changing their occupations, the total regional demand for the occupation is unaffected. When skilled workers change their occupations, the vacancies need to be filled by qualified unemployed jobseekers and fresh TVET graduates.
Accurate data on the flow of skilled workers quitting their jobs and aiming to change their occupations are challenging to produce. In practice, such data are not collected, and the labor turnover is not modelled.

Evidence indicates that the probability that a worker should be replaced after quitting a given occupation would strongly depend on the type of that occupation, education/qualification level, age of the worker, and tenure. The size of the occupational turnover and the resulting replacement demand can be very significant.

For example, data produced by the Job Openings and Labor Turnover Survey (JOLTS) conducted in the United States show considerable differences in replacement demand across industries, occupational groups, and seasons of the year.

Supply of skilled labor and related variables

Skilled labor is generally characterized by professional education (college and higher), possession of knowledge and skills to perform complicated tasks, ability to adapt quickly to technology changes, and creative application of knowledge and skills acquired through training in their work.

In essence, skilled workers are those directly and closely involved in the generation, development, spreading and application of knowledge.

TVET and tertiary graduates as part of skilled labor supply

Supply of skilled labor involves the following two major streams:

- TVET and tertiary graduates who completed their studies in a reference/base year and presumably joined the labor force in the year of graduation; and

- Skilled LFS unemployed.

The overall objective of a comprehensive LMI is to advise the regional TVET and tertiary education systems on the risks of under-and oversupply of graduates against the existing demand in the regional labor markets. The TVET and tertiary graduates and the professional education programs producing them are considered the only supply-side component, which could be monitored/managed by reviewing the enrolment and funding policies. Importantly, TVET and tertiary graduates are deemed to be skilled or technically educated by definition.

Data on the TVET and tertiary graduates are usually collected from databases of relevant national technical education authorities and higher education bodies and compared or complemented with information from other sources, including public and private providers. The key variables to be included are (a) the title and duration of the technical education program; (b) the occupation/field of study (for tertiary graduates); and (b) the NQF qualification level. In addition, the estimates of shares of TVET and tertiary graduates who joined the labor force in the year of graduation should also be produced.

TVET and tertiary graduates in full-time training at the time of a relevant statistical observation must be considered "not in the labor force". Consequently, the fresh supply of the TVET and tertiary graduates by occupation in a given year is counted as a sum of all graduates who completed their studies and joined the labor force in that year.

The LFS unemployed as part of the supply of skilled labor

The LFS unemployed are defined as all persons of working age who were not in employment, carried out activities to seek employment during a specified recent period, and were currently available to take up employment given a job opportunity. Since the analysis of demand and supply of labor focuses on skilled persons, the unskilled unemployed should be excluded from the calculation. Generally, an LFS provides the following information on the occupational structure of the unemployed:

- Occupation of unemployed persons with employment experience characterized either by the occupation in the last job (no matter how that occupation was acquired, including on-the-

job training) or the highest educational level and the field of professional education attained.
- Occupation of unemployed persons without previous employment experience attributed based on the highest educational level, and the field of professional education attained.

Notably, unemployed persons who did not have a skilled occupation in their last job and did not receive any professional education should be excluded from the calculation because they are considered unskilled.

The annual supply of skilled unemployed persons by occupation is counted based on the LFS yearly averages. The occupational structure of the unemployed is changing under the influence of labor market forces. Data series need to be produced following this stream of skilled labor supply in a regional labor market.

Practice shows that only a particular part of the unemployed in both streams of supply usually involve TVET and tertiary graduates. In contrast, a considerable share of labor supply is generally unskilled or low-skilled laborers.

For analysis of the supply side, which requires the identification of skilled unemployed by occupation among persons with previous employment experience, the following two variables are required:

- occupation in the last job (demonstrated previous experience or skills acquired in the last job); and
- the highest level of professional educational attainment, if any, which may lead to a particular occupation or a job.

Apparently, due to the labor market conditions, the occupation in the last job (field of occupation and qualification level) may differ from the highest level and the field of professional education attained.

By contrast, the unemployed who did not have any previous employment experience can only be characterized by their highest professional educational attainment (level and field of study), which can potentially lead to employment. Such unemployed persons may include the TVET and tertiary graduates who completed studies in the same year the LFS was conducted.

Conclusion

This Abstract paper has briefly described the key dimensions used for the occupational analysis of demand and supply of skilled labor, which is a cornerstone of comprehensive labor market information for TVET planning.

It has also described variables related to the supply of skilled labor such as TVET and tertiary graduates, and the LFS unemployed.

Particular attention has been placed on «replacement demand» for skilled labor.

As follows from the materials discussed, it is prudent to know the nature of future demand for skilled labor when determining the overall need for producing TVET graduates.

References:

- https://www.gov.nl.ca/labourmarketinformation/#:~:text=Labour%20market%20infor mation%2C%20or%20LM I,decisions%20about%20the%20labour%20market.
- https://www.gov.nl.ca/labourmarketinformation/#:~:text=Labour%20market%20inform ation%2C%20or%20LM I,decisions%20about%20the%20labour%20market.
- ILO Plolicy Brief. Vol.1 2024. Skilled Labor: A determining factor for sustainable growth of the nation (see available at: https://www.ilo.org/wcmsp5/groups/public/--- asia/---ro-bangkok/---ilo- hanoi/documents/publication/wcms_428969.pdf).
- 19th ICLS. Resolution concerning statistics of work, employment and labor underutilization (see available at: https://www.ilo.org/wcmsp5/groups/public/--- dgreports/---stat/documents/normativeinstrument/wcms_230304.pdf).
- Betcherman G., Olivas K., Dar A.: Impacts of active labor market programs: New evidence from evaluations with particular attention to developing and transition countries (Social Protection Discussion Paper Series No.0402). Washington: World Bank; 2004.
- Betcherman G., Godfrey M., Puerto S., Rother F., Staverska A.,: A Review of interventions to support young workers: Findings of the youth employment inventory (Social Protection Discuusion Paper No. 0715). Washington: World Bank: 2007;
- Chong A., Galdo J.: Does the Quality of training programs matter? Evidence from bidding processes data (IZA Discussion Paper No.2202). Bonn: Institute for the Study of Labor; 2006;
- Fares J., Puerto OS.: Towards comprehensive training (Social Protection Discussion Paper No.0924). Washington: World Bank; 2009;
- National Qualifications Framework – Georgian European Training Foundation. Working together Learning for life;
- TVET in Georgia

On Economic and Legal Aspects of Property

Abstract

The article deals with the issues of property as a fundamental economic category of the system of economic relations of societies. From the point of view of the methodology of analysis of property relations, economic and legal aspects are differentiated. In particular, in the first case, relations between subjects are implied in the process of production, distribution, exchange, and consumption of material goods (de facto), and in the second case, ownership (who owns what) (de jure). The economy (its functioning) is based on the actions of **objective** economic laws, while the law is based on **subjective** judgments and decisions. The privatization of property should not be an end in itself, but a way to effectively use the factors of production, which ultimately ensures economic growth. No form of ownership leads to an automatic increase in efficiency (the experience of post-Soviet reality has confirmed this). An analysis of the economics of crime and punishment is given.

Key words: Property; Economic and Legal Aspects of Property, Crime and Punishment

For citation: Beridze, T., & Ovsyannikova, N. (2022). On Economical and Legal Aspects of the Property. *Globalization and Business.* 13, 25-29. https://doi.org/10.35945/gb.2022.13.003

Introduction

Property, as a social phenomenon and property relationship, always occupied the minds of people and defined their actions for centuries (its analysis at the level of category, for example, relation, began as early as the seventeenth century: Francois Quesnay (Quesnay, 1766) - The theory of the sacred product, Victor Riqueti de Mirabeau (Mirabeau, 1901) - The role of nature factor in the economy, Ann Robert Jacques Turgot (Turgot, 1793) - How does the administrative system affect the economy? Property as an interdisciplinary phenomenon (the intersection of economics and law) received special attention in the 1930s (Coase, R.H. (1937), The

Nature of the Firm. Economica. 4 (16) 386-405. DOI: 10.1111 /j.1468-0335. 1937.tb00002.x).

What is the difference between these two social sciences in respect of property?

From the point of view of economic science - property means the relations that result in the creation of material wealth, its production, distribution, exchange, and consumption.

From the point of view of legal science, the following construction takes place - appropriation, possession, disposal, use. In other words, who owns what (legally registered, documentary).

Another feature that helps to understand the difference between the legal and economic aspects of the property is **its realization**, that is, **earning income** from its use.

Law and Economics interact in many ways. Whereas Private Law assists individuals and groups who are willing to enter into agreements in a free market, public law seeks to correct the outcomes of a free market system, using economic and social regulation. Law and Economics mesh together two of society's fundamental social constructs into one subject, allowing a multi-faceted study of significant problems which exist in each subject.

Law and Economics began its synthesis as a discipline through the theories of the Chicago School and received guidance and influence from such pioneers as Guido Calabresi (The Future of ..., 2016) and Nobel Prize winners Ronald Coase and Gary Becker. Richard Posner's book "Economic Analysis of Law" became one of the classic disciplines (Posner, 2011). Recently, other methods have moved to the fore, including the Property rights approach, the Austrian School, and the Neo-Institutionalist approach. Finally, the Public Choice School with Nobel Prize winner James Buchanan as an outstanding author focuses more specifically on the political context of the Law-making process.

The essential features of the economic analysis of law in modern perception include system for evaluating law and its institutions through the categories of efficiency, rationality and expediency (Cooter, Ulen, 2012). At the same time, in modern science, the economic analysis of law has two different meanings: on the one hand, it is defined as a method of research and evaluation of legal activity, and on the other hand, as a means of normative transformation. In general, the economic analysis of law is aimed at modifying the legal worldview, departing from the letter of the law, and is most often positioned by its supporters as "the key to a better law" in all legal systems.

The importance of the analysis of the above problems is multiplied in the "transition period" in the economy. To- day, after three decades since the beginning of the so-called "transition period" from a centrally controlled economy to a market economy, in the societies of countries that have made such a transition (and there are 27 such countries with a population of almost 300 million people), the questions about the correctness and effectiveness of the taken steps legitimately arise. Therefore, there is a need for an objective assessment of what we have received as a result of this socio-economic transformation in the post-socialist states. It should be recognized that there is **an objective need to develop a "theory of the transition economy", moreover, today we can already talk about the "post-transition economy".** Today, the development of such a theory in its significance can be compared with the development of the main theories in its time, both economic science and legal science (especially ownership rights). In the article, the terms "transitional economy" and "transformational economy" are used as synonyms, although there is a certain difference between them - the "transitional economy" refers to the movement from a centralized economy to a market economy, and "transformational" generally means significant shifts in any societies and economies, which took place in pre-capitalist formations as well.

One of the first capital studies on the transformational economy is the work by Karl Polanyi (Karl Polanyi, 1944) in which he studies the issues of Societies and Economic Systems, Evolution of the Market, Government and Market Economy, Social Change. The collective monographs (Islam & Mandelbaum, 1993) and Edward Lazear (Lazear, 1995) should also be noted. The first of them examines the transition from a planned economy to a market economy in Central and Eastern Europe, as well as in the former USSR, and the second one studies more specific issues (macroeconomics, privatization, interstate and fiscal relations, foreign trade, institutional reforms, employment, and unemployment).

The economy of the "transition period" has several specific characteristics that distinguish it from economies that are in a stationary state and develop **on their basis**. In particular, in a transition economy, new economic relations and new institutions are emerging that replace the old ones. As a result, new macro- and microeconomic patterns and trends, social and political changes, and new content of economic policy emerge. The search for intersection points and the identification of the basics of constructive interaction between the institutions of economics and law is an urgent task of economic and legal research. In general, it is correctly not-ed that the participants in social production act not only as carriers of property relations, and production relations but also as legal subjects.

The economy (its functioning) is based on the actions of objective economic laws, while the law is based on subjective judgments and decisions. In other words, in the first case, we have a positive approach to the analysis of socio-economic realities, and in the second, a normative one.

The economic and legal aspects of ownership: unity and difference

Property is, firstly, an economic category that reflects the relations between people regarding things, and secondly, a certain relationship that is subject to legal regulation. Accordingly, the following contents of ownership are distinguished: economic and legal.

Economic theory tends to take the functioning of the system of property and contract for granted and focuses on the operation of the price mechanism (microeconomics).

The economic essence of property is built on the relationship between the subject (owner) and the object (property). As a rule, the property is a property on which the pro- duction process depends - economic resources, factors of production. From the economic point of view, only such objects can be called property that is capable of either generating income for their owners or directly satisfying their needs. The main forms of realization of property are **possession, disposal, and use**.

The possession is understood as the actual possession of the property, which implies the right to sell, grant, or bequeath, as well as to destroy or dispose of this property.

The disposal implies the right to change a thing, rent it out, or use it as collateral.

The use means the extraction of useful properties of the object of property in the process of consumption or earning of income.

All these three forms of realization of the property clearly show how the economic and legal content of property are
interconnected and turn into each other.

The legal essence of property presupposes the rules of property regulation generally accepted at the legislative lev- el. Legal relations are the formally attached rights and obligations concerning the property, while economic relations are the actual relations to the object of property (for example, the costs of its maintenance, or the benefit from its use).

If the legal aspect corresponds to the categories of "appropriation - disposal" or "possession", then the economic aspect of the relationship corresponds to the creation of material wealth and its use (effectiveness). In the first case, the main content is that the object of property belongs to the subject **(what to whom)**, **de jure** - to the state, a group of persons, an individual (here we recall the postulate in the well-known Coase Theorem: it is not so important how the property is distributed, it is important that property rights were recorded), in the second case - the economic one - the main thing is the efficiency of using this object (**what and how**), **de facto**. In other words, **for a lawyer, the form of be- longing is important; belonging is more important for the legal aspect than for the economic one, and for an economist - it's content (getting benefits, income**). Property in the economy is social relations within the framework of ownership, separation, and redistribution of property objects. The economic content of property is revealed through ownership, management, and control. The right of ownership is a set of legal norms that fix the appropriation of things to individuals and groups. Ownership is the actual possession of the property. Use is the extraction of useful properties from the property, such as income. That is why privatization, which is the main means and form of ownership change, should not become an end in itself during the transition to the market, but only be its tool in creating an effective owner.

Property rights are the constructs in economics for determining how a resource or economic good is used and owned (Alchian, 2008). Resources can be owned by (and hence be the property of) individuals, associations, collectives, or governments (Alchian, 2008).

An important feature of property relations is the diversity of its forms. Such an approach to the analysis of property relations was characteristic of the so-called "perestroika period" of the late USSR. At the same time, all forms of ownership were recognized as equivalent, and this seemed almost an achievement in the theory of economic thought?! Meanwhile, following the logic of the obligatory allocation of a core in property relations, it must be recognized that the **dominant** form of property relations in a transitional economy (as well as in a "post-transitional" one, by the way) are private-property relations (in various forms of their manifestation - joint-stock, group, individual) that lay the foundations for future economies.

An important aspect of ownership is its connection to the efficiency of production. None of the forms of ownership automatically leads to an increase in the efficiency of the economy (the results of post-Soviet privatization have convinced us of this. It is necessary to have appropriate institutions (a formal – the state institutions and an informal – the social background, mentality, thinking, culture, religion, etc.), which will promote the full realization of the potential of this or that form of ownership.

Here we want to make a retrospective journey into the history of the Georgian economy: along with economic growth in Georgia, the replacement of the form of ownership (public to private) had several specific aspects to consider in assessing the place of private property, its scale of effective- ness and dynamics.

First, the economic theory did not develop a unified theoretical-conceptual model of such a transition in the early 1990s, when the process of systemic transformation into a market economy began, with the criteria of fairness applicable to the mass privatization of the means of production. Everything was based on the weight of the local political forces, the views, the opportunistic approaches to the current situation, and the use of the method of "trial and error".

Second, in contrast to Central and Eastern European countries, the situation in Georgia, as in most post-Soviet countries, was much worse and more dramatic. The countries of Central and Eastern Europe needed only a change of ownership, the denationalization in the conditions of maintaining a unified economic organism, and the internal trans- formation of property relations in it. In Georgia, the transformation of property relations took place in the qualitatively new conditions of a total breakdown of old, traditional eco- nomic ties and the formation of a new systemic unity. To take an honest look, during the Soviet era the Georgian economy did not exist as a united mechanism - it was a set of "N" enterprises located on the territory of Georgia, cooperating with enterprises from other regions of the USSR outside Georgia. According to the 1987 interbranch balance of production and distribution of Georgian products, the total value of imports and exports of products exceeded 130 percent of gross domestic product (GDP). The cost of products exported abroad by Georgian machine-building enterprises reached ¾ of the total output of these enterprises; almost 3/5 of Georgia's im- ports and export came to the Russian Federation.

The instantaneous breakdown of such connections caused enormous damage to the economy, which in the early 1990s alone had more than 100 enterprises and industries. Under the directive rule, Georgia was guaranteed to receive raw materials and key markets, so diversifying production under such conditions was even considered a priority. But it was the breakdown of such binding ties that showed the fragility of such an "advantage." Georgia faced the world economy head-to-head and it turned out that the country had no high-demand assets, in fact, liquid goods (for example, energy carriers such as Turkmenistan and Azerbaijan). Georgian tea and citrus, which accounted for 9/10 of the total consumption of the USSR in the conditions of the Soviet economic system, were swiftly substituted on the Russian market. By 1994, the country's gross domestic product had fallen 3.9 times compared to 1988 (the best year in terms of economic performance before the reform), industry output had fallen six times or more, and the number of hired workers had fallen by 1.7 million people in the same period, in the conditions of the reduction of the total population of the country "only" by 400 thousand people; the well-being of the population has been thrown back by several decades.

Indeed, the duration of the economic downturn in Georgia during the transition to a market economy was quite long (about 71 months, from the fourth quarter of 1988 to August 1994), while in the Baltic states, for example, it lasted only 25-27 months and the cumulative economic decline was 23 percent. But we repeat: if not for private property-based market relations, the Georgian economy would be in a much more difficult, backward, unfavorable situation. It is the private property economy of Georgia, thanks to the smooth and efficient work of state institutions, that despite the global economic crisis and the war with Russia (August 2008), the country's gross domestic product (GDP) in 2009 decreased only by 3.9 percent compared to the previous year, while in 2010 it exceeded the level of 2008 (by 2.1 percent) (data based on data from the National Statistics Office of Georgia). In general, the form of ownership, the private property should be considered as a necessary but insufficient condition for economic growth. The following factors are also to be taken into account:

a) high motivation of the social forces of the society in the economic results;

b) balancing all factors of production according to their potential;

c) existence of relevant key markets, for example, growth of demand (competitiveness of the economy). Therefore, the eco- nomic collapse in Georgia in the first half of the 1990s was largely caused by the fact that the production profile adjust- ed to the old paradigm was inconsistent with the free market relations and economic ties; however surmounting the crisis by the country in the shortest period has been stipulated by the liberty of business and the liberal policy, which started and is being implemented by the Georgian government following the recommendations of international economic and financial institutions (IMF, World Bank).

The Crime and Punishment: An Economic Approach

In this sketch, we want to pay attention to the economic aspect of crime and punishment, in other words, to conduct some economic analysis of law. Note, insofar as they are connected specifically with property, property relations (we do not touch on intellectual property - this is a separate subject of study).

In general, the disclosure of the economic approach to crime and punishment once again confirms the relationship between jurisprudence and economic disciplines, and only in the interaction points of these two disciplines can one achieve significant scientific and practical results, both in one and another branch of science. In the words of the Nobel laureate in economics Gary Becker, "the economic approach is all-encompassing; it applies to all behavior". Here, in our opinion, one can also mean the behavioral logic of criminals, although almost not studied by economists.

What do we understand by the economic content of crime and punishment? This is, of course, first of all, the statistics of crimes recorded by the statistical divisions of government structures; behind the figures, there is a wide variety of crimes – from small ones to large criminal cases. So, it is early to cherish hopes for the law-abiding population.

Let us start with the crimes. First, it is well-known, crimes are committed for several reasons: a pathological ad- diction to perpetrate a crime (psychopathy); the second; the second is kleptomania (a special disease for thieving); third – economic malfeasance in office (corruption); and finally, the fourth – economic caused by unemployment, lack of income, low standard of living (incomes should at least be equal to the subsistence minimum per person on average). For ex- ample, in Georgia: the subsistence minimum for a man able to work in November 2021 was 223.7 GEL, and the average monthly nominal salary was – 1328 GEL).

As for the expenditure, significant public and private funds are spent on preventing and catching criminals. The optimal cost of law enforcement depends, among other things, on the cost of catching violators and establishing their guilt, on the type of punishment – for example, whether fines or imprisonment are applied – and on the reaction of criminals to changes in the law enforcement system. Thus, the conversation inevitably touches on issues related to penology (the science of punishment) and other theories of criminal behavior.

Five types of relationships can be distinguished that give an idea of the costs: 1) the number of offenses and the costs associated with them; 2) the number of crimes and the severity of punishment; 3) the number of crimes that ended in the capture of criminals and the establishment of their guilt, on the one hand, and budget expenditures for the maintenance of the police and the judicial system, on the other; 4) the number of crimes that ended in the capture of criminals and the establishment of their guilt, and the costs of keeping criminals in places of deprivation of liberty and for the implementation of punishment in other forms; 5) the number of offenses and the costs of the private sector to ensure their security and to detain criminals.

As for the punishment (economic aspect) – the costs of maintaining the policy of criminal courts and lawyers in criminal cases for the maintenance of correctional labor institutions at the expense of the budgets of all levels of prisons. The costs of a criminal associated with various types of punishments can be brought to a comparable form by con- verting them into a monetary equivalent, where only fines are directly-measured from all punishments. For example, incarceration for a criminal is the discounted amount of lost earnings plus how much he estimates his damage from imprisonment and life on a meager action.

Punishments affect not only criminals but also other members of society: first of all, the family members of the offender – after all, they lose part of their income due to the absence of the guilty one of the family members.

The total cost of punishment for the whole society is the sum of the cost of punishment for criminals and the gain or loss associated with this punishment for the rest of society. Fines are levied on offenders from the income of the rest of society, which is equal to the loss of the offender minus the cost of imposing a fine, so the cost of society in connection with the fines is approximately zero, as it should be in the case of a social transfer (Becker, 2003).

Generally, improvements in economic conditions, such as lower unemployment and higher wages, play an important role in reducing crime.

Finally, we emphasize that since societies develop dynamically, the economic and legal systems develop along with them, and it is too early to make a final study of this issue, so this issue will never be closed.

BIBLIOGRAPHY

Alchian, A. (2008). Property rights in David R. Henderson (ed.). Concise Encyclopedia of Economics (2nd ed.). Indianapolis: Library of Economics & Liberty. ISBN 978-0-86597-665-8. OCLC 237794267.

Alchian, A. A. (2008). Property Rights. New Palgrave Dictionary of Economics, Second edition.

Becker, G. S. (2003). Selected Works on Economic Theory. Human Behavior. Economical Approach. Moscow. High School of Economics (HSE).

Calabresi, G. (2016). The Future of Law and Economics: Essays in Reform and Recollection. ISBN-13: 9780300195897 Yale University DOI: 10.12987/Yale/9780300195897.001.0001

Coase, R. H. (1937). The Nature of the Firm. *Economica.* 4 (16). https://onlinelibrary.wiley.com/doi/10.1111/j.1468-0335.1937. tb00002.x

Cooter, R., & Ulen, T. (2012). Law and Economics. Boston: Addison-Wesley. 10-34; 70-73.

Economic Transition in Eastern Europe and Russia. Realities of Reform. Edited by Edward P. Lazear (1995) Hoover Institution Press. Stanford University. Stanford California.

François Quesnay (Juin 1766). Analyse de la formule arithmétique du tableau economique de la distribution des depenses annuelles d'une Nation Agricole. *Journal de l'Agriculture, du Commerce et des Finances.* 2(3), 11-41.

Le Marquis de Mirabeau. (1901). Ses Theories Politiques et Economiques, (These pour le Doctoral) Paris.

Making Markets. Economic Transformation in Eastern Europe and the Post-Soviet States. Ed. by Shafiqul Islam and Michael Mandelbaum (1993) Council on Foreign Relations Press. New York.

Posner, R. A. (2011). Wolters Kluwer. Austin Boston Chicago New York the Netherlands. 3-36.

The Great Transformation. The Political and Economic Origins of our time. Karl Polanyi. Beacon Press Boston. 1944; second edition 1957.

Turgot, A. R. J. (1793). Reflections on the Formation and Distribution of Wealth. London: Printed by E. Spragg, for J. Good, Book- seller, 159. New Bond Street; John Anderson, 62, Holborn Hill; and W. Richardson, Royal.

a) Since TVET produces skilled workforce, the "additional demand" will focus only on technically trained/educated workforce in employment, while the semi-skilled and unskilled labor are commonly excluded from calculations.

b) A National Qualification Framework referring to job titles corresponding to national qualification types/levels (NQF). Analysis of demand for skilled workforce involves the following key variables:

- *employment in each skilled occupation* in the region across all industries in the base year;
- *anticipated future dynamics of employment by industry and occupations* in that industry;
- *the number of unfilled vacancies by occupation* by the end of each reference period (quarter or year) and anticipation of future trends.

Demand for skilled labor

There are the following two concepts of demand

- «Aggregate demand for skilled labor» - usually used for planning and projections - the total size of the labor force (by occupational group) required or anticipated in a country in a given year.
- «Additional demand for skilled labor" – used for TVET delivery planning - a number of the skilled labor force by occupation that requires to be reproduced annually by the system of professional education (nationally and in a region).

TVET system will have to take account of the anticipated increase or decrease of the labor force in industries to replenish the labor force who will retire, change their occupation or exit the labor force for other reasons.

Skilled employment in each occupation is the basis for the calculation of the demand for this occupation. The number of unfilled vacancies by occupation demonstrates shortages of labor or the influence of some factors of the workplace (wages/working conditions);

The anticipated short-term demand for skilled labor

www.ingramcontent.com/pod-product-compliance
Lightning Source LLC
LaVergne TN
LVHW022304200926
848481LV00004B/1217

* 9 7 9 8 8 9 2 4 8 4 0 6 0 *